the
book
of
buns

the
book
of
buns

Over 50 brilliant bakes
from around the world

Jane Mason

photography by Peter Cassidy

RYLAND PETERS & SMALL
LONDON • NEW YORK

To Enrique who loves my buns.

Senior Designer Sonya Nathoo
Senior Editor Miriam Catley
Picture Researcher Christina Borsi
Production Manager Toby Marshall
Art Director Leslie Harrington
Editorial Director Julia Charles

Prop Stylist Joanna Harris
Food Stylists Rosie Reynolds,
Kathy Kordalis and Emily Kydd
US Recipe Tester Susan Stuck
Indexer Hilary Bird

First published in 2013 by
Ryland Peters & Small
20–21 Jockey's Fields, London WC1R 4BW
and
519 Broadway, 5th Floor, New York, NY 10012
www.rylandpeters.com

10 9 8 7 6 5 4 3 2 1

Text © Jane Mason 2013.
Design and photographs ©
Ryland Peters & Small 2013.

ISBN: 978-1-84975-435-4

A CIP record for this book is available from
the British Library.
A CIP record for this book is available from the
US Library of Congress.

Notes
• All spoon measurements are level
unless otherwise specified.
• All eggs are medium (UK) or large (US)
unless otherwise specified.
• Ovens should be preheated to the specified
temperatures. All ovens work slightly differently.
We recommend using an oven thermometer
and suggest you consult the maker's handbook
for any special instructions, particularly if you
are cooking in a fan-assisted/convection oven,
as you will need to adjust temperatures
according to manufacturer's instructions.

Printed and bound in China

Contents

A bun's a bun the world around

There are hamburger buns and hot dog buns; hot cross buns and iced buns; steamed buns and sticky buns; cinnamon buns and coconut buns. There are thousands of kinds of buns – sweet and savoury, for celebrations and as daily bread – from almost every corner of the world.

The origin of the word bun is unknown. Although it came into use in English in the Middle Ages as a word that indicates a loaf of bread as big as a fist, the reality is that buns have been around for a while. The earliest evidence that we have of the existence of buns is from ancient Egypt where drawings depict the ancient Egyptians baking and eating buns. However, there is no reason to believe that the Egyptians were the first people to bake buns – we have probably been baking them for as long as we have been baking bread.

Why was the bun born? It could be that some people just did not want to share their food – they wanted their very own little loaf of bread and so the bun was invented. It could also be that – way back when we were just using coarsely ground wholemeal/whole-wheat flour and water to make buns – buns were easier to shape and they certainly took less time in the oven. Alternatively, it could be that a bun – as a single portion of bread completely surrounded by crust – is easier to transport and stays fresh longer than sliced bread.

Although we do not know what led to the invention of buns, we do know the variety is endless and their popularity and place on our table is enduring.

BUN INGREDIENTS

Flour

Most of the buns in this book are baked with white wheat flour. Each recipe will tell you if you need plain/all-purpose flour or strong (bread) flour. If you are committed to wholemeal/whole-wheat flour, please use it. The buns will taste stronger and be slightly smaller and less airy. If you are committed to spelt flour (either white or whole) please use it. Whatever flour you choose, you may have to adjust the amount of water or flour ever so slightly (we are talking grams here) because from bag to bag and grain to grain, flour is always different.

Many of the recipes will guide you regarding whether you should expect a particularly dry or wet dough. Don't panic when the dough is stickier than you are used to. Keep calm and keep kneading.

Yeast

There are three different kinds of yeast called for in this book: instant, dry or fresh. Instant yeast (also called easy bake) looks like a powder. Dry yeast looks like little, round pellets. Fresh yeast looks like a beige eraser. Every recipe tells you how much of each kind of yeast to use and how to use it. So no matter what kind of yeast you can buy near you, be assured, you can use it with confidence.

Fats

Many of the recipes in this book call for butter and many call for lard. If you are an omnivore please follow the recipes. Contrary to popular belief, lard is not bad for you when eaten in moderation. In fact, it is positively good for you and is lower in saturated fat than butter. As ever, buy the best lard you can find and the way to do this is to order it from a good butcher. The lard you can buy at most supermarkets is highly refined and lacking in flavour – just like most butter, by the way.

Butter is not a perfect substitute for lard because butter separates into solids and liquids when it melts. When you use butter, knead it in at the end of the kneading process to avoid it melting before it is absorbed into the flour. Using cold butter and cutting it into little cubes helps.

If you are a vegan or simply don't eat dairy, you can substitute a good-quality neutral fat for the butter or the lard. Coconut oil, avocado oil and grape seed oil are reasonably neutral oils and make reasonably neutral substitutes. Olive oil simply has too strong a flavour to be a good substitute for butter or lard. There will always be a taste and performance tradeoff, just so you know.

Water

Use water from the cold tap. That way you never need to worry about killing the yeast by using water that is too warm.

Milk

Use full-fat milk when you are baking buns. Milk enriches and softens the dough and provides great flavour. There is flavour in the fat and, believe me, you will taste and feel the difference.

Other delicious things

Many recipes call for chopped nuts, dried fruit, fresh herbs, diced vegetables, etc. When adding things like this to the dough, follow the instructions and add them once you have kneaded your dough and allow it to rest for a while. This way you can squish in the delicious things you are adding without destroying them or hurting your hands. The dough will recover.

WORKING WITH YOUR DOUGH

Kneading

Once you have mixed all the ingredients in the bowl according to the recipe, scrape the dough directly onto a clean surface and knead it for a good 10 minutes or as stated in the recipe. Gluten is like a balloon and the first thing you do to a balloon before you blow it up is stretch it so you can blow it up more easily. Kneading is the same. It is simply stretching, and you can stretch the dough any way you like: one-handed, two-handed, in the air, with your knuckles or using a dough scraper, folding the dough over and over. Just be sure you give the dough a good stretch for at least 10 minutes. If you are using a machine, use the dough hook and check every few minutes that the flour is being scooped off the bottom of the bowl. You may need to get in there with a scraper to turn the dough over several times, depending on the recipe. That is fine – don't worry about it – just make sure all the flour is being kneaded in by the machine. It's worthwhile to knead by hand the first time you do a recipe so you can feel for the texture the recipe seeks. Please don't be tempted to add more flour to any of the recipes. Sticky is good. Err on the side of sticky rather than on the side of dry.

Rising

You need to allow the dough to rise at various stages and this information will always be laid out in the individual recipes. If your kitchen is cold, your dough will move slowly and, conversely, if your kitchen is warm, your dough will move quickly. Dough with a high fat content takes much longer to rise than dough with no fat at all so don't worry if your high butter dough is sitting around for four or even six hours. As long as the yeast is alive, the dough will rise. During the first and the final rise (in the bowl and on the baking sheet) you want your dough to double in size unless directed otherwise in the recipe.

A couple of things to bear in mind:

1. If the buns significantly more than double in size during the final rise, they risk using up all the power in the yeast before they are baked and they may collapse when they get into the oven. If you spot that your buns have over-risen before you bake them, don't panic. Pull them off the baking sheet and knead a little bit more flour into them. Shape them again and put them back to rise.

2. If dough has not risen enough, it will split in the oven. It splits along the bottom where the baking sheet meets the bun. Chalk it up to experience and be a bit more patient next time.

Covering dough for rising

Covering your dough will prevent it from drying out while it rises. When dough is doing its first rise, in the bowl, cover it with clingfilm/plastic wrap, a plastic shower hat or a damp tea towel. Make sure the dough does not touch (and stick to) whatever is covering it. During the subsequent rises, the recipes will guide you regarding how best to cover your dough.

Pulling risen dough out of the bowl

When the dough has finished its first rise and you take it out of the bowl to start shape it, take it out gently. The recipes will state whether you should take it out onto a floured or an unfloured surface. Either way, please don't 'knock it back'. The dough has lots of lovely air in it and in most cases you want to keep it that way. Some recipes call for the dough to be rolled flat with a rolling pin, in which case you don't need to be so gentle.

BAKING YOUR BUNS

Most buns are cooked at a high temperature for a short time. You will see that most of the sweet buns are cooked at 220°C (425°F) Gas 7 for around 15 minutes and most of the savoury buns are cooked at either 220°C (425°F) Gas 7 or even 230°C (450°F) Gas 8 for around 20 minutes. However, ovens are different, temperatures vary and altitude plays a role in how quickly things take to bake. To that end, when you are doing a recipe for the first time, watch out! It could take a few more minutes, or a few less. Check it after

10 minutes or so and put a sheet of aluminium foil or baking parchment over the buns if they are getting too brown. Always use a good-quality, heavy baking sheet or pan to ensure the buns don't burn on the bottom. To prepare your baking sheets, line them with non-stick parchment paper.

All of the buns should sound hollow when you tap them on the bottom at the end of the baking time. If not, put them back for 2–3 more minutes.

THE RULES OF LIGHT, SOFT BUNS

If you want firm buns, go to the gym. The joy of buns is the fluffy, soft squashiness of them. To get light, soft buns there are some rules.

1. Make a predough if it is called for in the recipe. Predoughs of any kind soften, lighten and add richness and flavour to the final dough.

2. When asked, heat the milk to just below boiling point and allow it cool down to room temperature. You do this to denature certain of the milk proteins, thus helping the bread to achieve a better rise. Let the milk cool right down before adding it to the dough or the heat will kill the yeast. Heat the milk several hours (or the night) before you bake, and allow it to sit on the counter to cool right down.

3. Knead according to the instructions in the recipe whether you are kneading by hand or by machine. Knead in the butter last when you are asked to – and knead it for the full amount of time stated.

4. Don't allow the dough to rise in the fridge unless called to do so. Dough that rises in a cool environment over time is a little sturdier than dough that is not.

5. Do be patient with your dough. Dough with a high butter content, for example, can take hours and hours to rise.

6. Don't over-flour. Too much flour equals heavy buns.

7. Don't squash air out of dough unless you are asked to do so. Learn to shape the dough gently once it has risen. The days of 'knocking back' are over.

8. Heat slightly more milk than you need and then measure it again just before adding it. Milk seems to disappear when it's heated.

You do not have to follow these rules. Your buns will still be delicious, just not as light.

A NOTE FOR FANS OF SOURDOUGH

You can replace yeast with sourdough if you like. Double the amount of fresh yeast called for and use that quantity of rye starter. Quadruple it for a wheat starter. Refresh the starter with 25 percent of the flour and 25 percent of the liquid called flour and then pretend this is your 'yeast'. Complete the recipe, using the remaining ingredients, and at least doubling the resting time at every stage.

Basic shaping techniques

Shaping is the true art of the baker – and really the only tricky thing about baking buns. Within reason, dough is dough but the infinite number of shapes and variations is proof of the creativity and skill of bakers throughout the ages.

Anyone can knead dough but shaping takes practice. From a visual perspective you have to transform the blob of dough in your mixing bowl into something lovely that keeps its shape while it rises again and bakes. From a technical perspective you have to try to give that blob of dough structure without squeezing all the air out of it. Don't panic. You can do it. Just be patient and buy a plastic scraper (available at most cooking stores) because it may change your life.

Stretching and folding the dough

There are plenty of ways to shape dough. This is only one way and if you have another way that works for you – use it! Before shaping your dough into a sausage or a ball you will be called to stretch and fold the dough. Pretend the blob of dough is a clock. Starting at noon, gently pinch about 1 cm/½ inch of the edge of the dough and pull it away from the blob, stretching it as far as you can without breaking it. Don't worry if you do, just try not to. Fold that pinched bit right back over the blob and gently lay it down. Repeat this action all around the blob of dough, essentially stacking it on itself. As you do it, you can turn the blob of dough, or move yourself around it. Using a scraper helps.

After this, the recipes take over, directing you how to deal with the dough to get the shape required. Of course, there are exceptions to the 'stretch and fold' starting point and they will be clearly indicated. You may, for example, be asked to pull the dough out before stuffing it or portion it out immediately.

Dividing the dough

Many of the recipes say, 'divide the dough into 10 equal portions' (or 12 portions or 20 portions or whatever). The easiest way to do this is to weigh the dough after its first rise and jot down how much it weighs. Divide the weight of the dough by the number of pieces you are asked to make and you will know how much each piece should weigh. 50 g/2 oz makes a small bun, 75 g/3 oz makes a medium sized bun, 100 g/4 oz makes a big bun. Just so you know!

Shaping a loose sausage and a tight sausage

Many recipes will call for you to shape a loose or a tight sausage to prepare the dough for being cut into bun portions. This intermediate step gives the dough new food and air, and forms a temporary structure that helps the dough continue to rise to enable you to get a light bun.

To shape a loose sausage:

A loose sausage is an intermediary shape in the preparation of some of the buns in this book. Stretch and fold the dough (see page 10). [1, 2] Gently roll the dough up on the spot into a sausage shape. [3] Allow it to rest as instructed in the recipe.

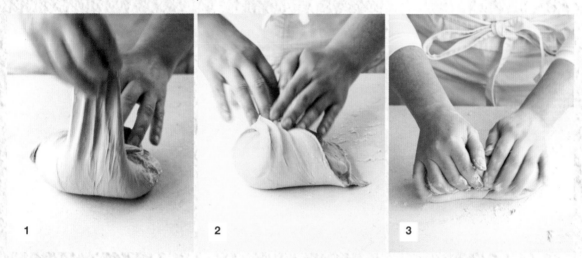

To shape a tight sausage:

Stretch and fold the dough (see page 10). [1, 2] Roll the dough up tightly. Use your fingers to tuck the dough in as you roll and use your palms to stretch and shape the sausage. You should end up with a little footstool of dough. [3]

Shaping a loose ball and a tight ball

Lots of buns are shaped liked balls. Whilst it is easier to shape a tight ball with drier dough, don't be alarmed when you are asked to shape a ball out of sticky dough. Flour your hands and roll with intent. With 10 or 12 individual balls to roll you will quickly become a master.

To shape a loose ball:
Stretch and fold the dough (see page 10). [1] Gently roll the dough up into a loose sausage and tuck the ends under to make a ball. [2] Allow to rest. [3]

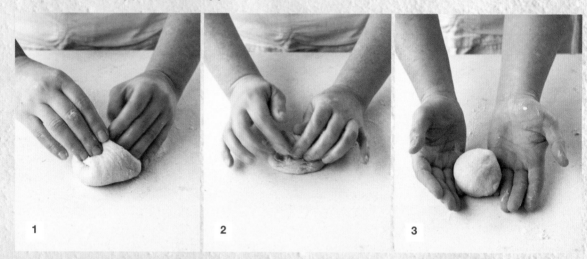

To shape a tight ball (dry dough):
Stretch and fold the dough (see page 10). [1] Flip the dough over and, using both hands, gently pull down and around the dough so your little fingers meet under the bottom of the dough ball. [2] Keep rotating the dough ball slightly and repeat the pulling action until you have formed a tight ball of dough. [3]

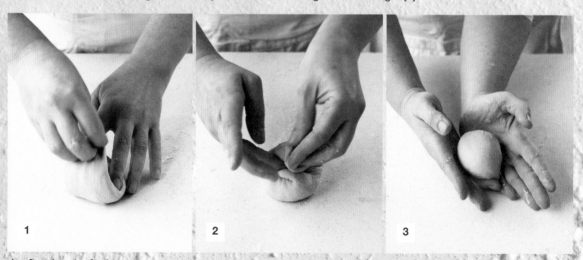

To shape a tight ball (sticky dough):

Scrape the dough out of the bowl. [1] Divide the dough into the number of portions indicated in the recipe and flour your hands. [2] Cup one hand over the dough with your fingertips on the table and your palm touching the dough – don't press down. [3] Move your hand around in a circle, keeping your fingers on the table and your palm on the dough. Use the table – and the fact that the dough is sticking to the table – to create the tension to pull the surface of the dough around itself. [4] Lift the sticky dough ball with a scraper to move it around. [5]

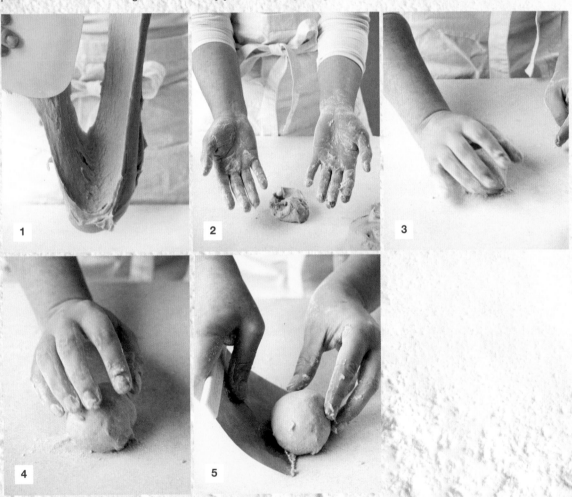

Filling and shaping swirly whirly and stuffed buns

Stuffed buns make an appearance all over the world. You can fill a bun with anything that takes your fancy – from ham to jam – and shape it into an impressive swirly whirly wheel, an oblong or ball. Don't use too much stuffing or your dough will be stretched too thinly, risking scorching or bursting. When making stuffed buns, if you find your dough is a little dry and the edges are not sticking together around the filling, simply wet the edges with water (or milk or egg).

To fill and shape a swirly whirly bun:
Roll the dough flat. [1] Spread the filling on top of the dough. [2] Roll the dough up tightly. [3] Slice it into pieces and then transfer to a prepared baking sheet. [4, 5]

To fill and shape an oblong:

Roll each portion of dough into a small disc. [1] Place a spoonful of filling on top. [2] Pinch the edges closed tightly so the bun does not open as it rises and bakes. [3]

1   2   3

To fill and shape a ball:

Roll each portion of dough into a small disc and put a spoonful of filling on top. Pleat the edges and gather them together around the filling to make a little parcel. [1, 2] Rest the buns pleated-side-up if called for. Alternatively, turn the bun over and seal the edges tightly with both hands resting the buns pleated-side-down. [3]

1   2   3

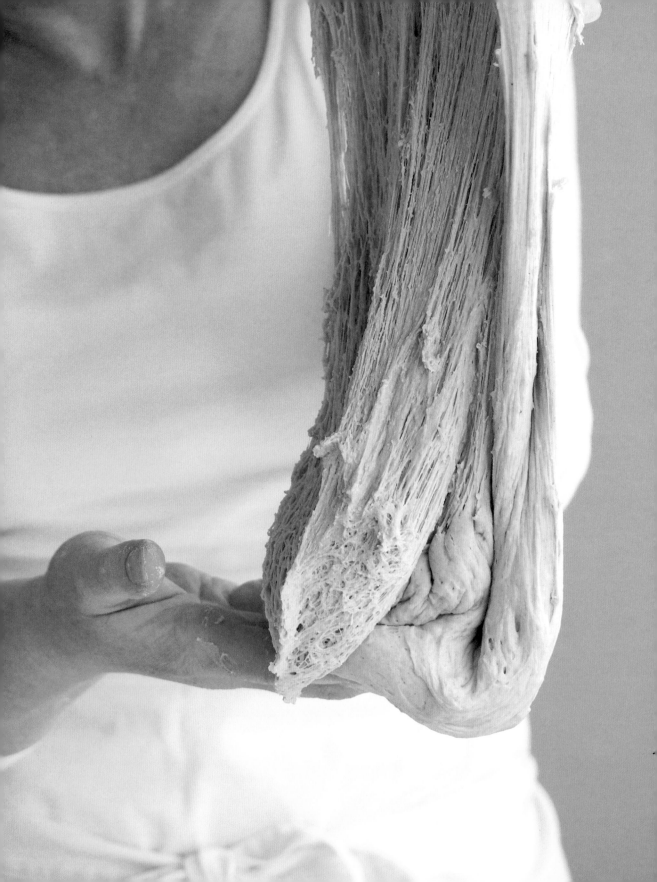

Everyday
Buns

Snittsidan Bullar Sweden

'Snittsidan' means 'cut side' in Swedish. Snittsidan Bullar are buns that are cut rather than rolled and this technique gives the buns their unique shape. To that end, this recipe is all about technique and you can try the technique with any bun recipe you like. This one is pretty good though.

250 g/2 cups strong (bread) flour (white, wholemeal/whole-wheat, spelt or a mixture)

50 g/⅓ cup plus 1 tablespoon rye flour (dark or light)

1.5 g/¾ teaspoon instant yeast, 3 g/1 teaspoon dry yeast, or 6 g/0.2 oz fresh yeast

220 g/1 scant cup water

6 g/1½ teaspoons salt

Decoration
seeds of your choice

Glaze
olive oil

prepared baking sheets (see page 9)

Makes 8 buns

If you are using instant or fresh yeast, put all the ingredients in a big bowl and mix them together. Pull the dough out of the bowl and knead for 10 minutes. The dough will be sticky because of the rye. Don't worry about it and do not add any more flour.

If you are using dry yeast, put the flour into a big bowl and make a well. Sprinkle the yeast into the well and add the water. Cover with a dry tea towel and allow to rest for 10–15 minutes. You may or may not get a beige sludge on the top of the water, but don't worry – what is important is to dissolve the yeast. Add the salt and mix all the ingredients together. Pull the dough out of the bowl and knead for 10 minutes. The dough will be sticky because of the rye. Don't worry about it and do not add any more flour.

Return the dough to the bowl, cover and allow to rest for 1–2 hours.

Pull the dough out gently onto an unfloured surface.

Shaping

Roll the dough into a tight sausage (see page 11). Cut a slice off the sausage about 2.5 cm/1 inch thick. Dip the 'cut side' of the slice (the cut sides are sticky) into a bowl of seeds and place it, seeds facing up, on the prepared baking sheet. Repeat with the remaining dough.

Cover with a dry tea towel and allow to rest for 45 minutes. The dough will not really rise as there is no top structure but it will get kind of holey and interesting.

Preheat the oven to 220°C (425°F) Gas 7.

Pop the buns in the preheated oven and bake for 20 minutes. Remove from the oven and transfer to a wire rack. Glaze the buns with olive oil when they are still hot before allowing them to cool completely. They make great sandwiches.

Krentenbollen Holland

Krentenbollen are practically the national dish in The Netherlands alongside cheese, pickled herring, Indonesian food and a number of other things. The key to a good Krentenbollen is to add plenty of raisins. You want a raisin bun, not a bun with raisins.

250 g/1 cup milk
1 tablespoon sugar
grated zest of 1 lemon
grated zest of 1 orange
400 g/3¼ cups plain/
    all-purpose white
    wheat flour
2 g/1 teaspoon instant
    yeast, 4 g/1¼ teaspoons
    dry yeast, or 8 g/0.28 oz
    fresh yeast
8 g/2 teaspoons salt
50 g/3 tablespoons butter,
    cubed, at room
    temperature
400 g/3⅓ cups dark
    raisins (or sultanas/
    golden raisins, whatever
    you fancy or have to
    hand) soaked in water
    or the alcohol of your
    choice overnight, or
    while your dough is
    resting if you have
    forgotten to soak them
    the night before

Glaze
1 egg
1 tablespoon water
1 teaspoon sugar
pinch of salt

*prepared baking sheets
    (see page 9)*

Makes 12 buns

Pour the milk into a little saucepan and add the sugar. Add the lemon zest and orange zest and bring it to boiling point, stirring all the while to dissolve the sugar. Allow to cool down completely.

Put the flour into a big mixing bowl and make a well in it. Sprinkle the yeast into the well and pour in the cooled milk. Flick some flour on the milk to close the well. Cover and allow to rest for 1 hour.

Add the salt and bring all the dough together in the bowl. Turn the dough out onto the counter and knead well for 10 minutes. The dough will be quite stiff. Add the butter and knead again for 10 minutes. Put it back in the bowl, cover and allow to rest for 30 minutes.

Drain the raisins (drink the liquid if it makes you happy) and dump them on top of the dough in the bowl. Work them in gently so that you don't squash them. Don't worry about the dough – it will be fine. Worry about the raisins. Once the raisins are worked in, cover the bowl again and allow the dough to rest for 2 hours.

Pull the dough out gently onto an unfloured surface.

Shaping
Shape the dough into a tight sausage (see page 11). Cut the sausage into 12 equal portions and allow them to rest under a dry tea towel for 15 minutes. Shape each portion into a tight ball (see page 12) and place the balls on the prepared baking sheet. Cover with a dry tea towel and allow them to rest for 30 minutes.

Flatten each ball slightly with your hand to a height of about 3 cm/1¼ inches. Beat together the ingredients for the glaze and paint the buns generously with the glaze. Allow to rest, uncovered, for 15 minutes.

Preheat the oven to 220°C (425°F) Gas 7.

Pop the buns in the preheated oven and bake for 15 minutes. Remove from the oven and allow to cool completely on a wire rack.

Muesli Stangen Germany

Stangen translates as 'rods'. Not a gorgeous name but definitely a gorgeous bun. Juicy and tasty, someone once told me that these were the best buns they had ever eaten. Please, I beg you, throw away those ghastly cereal bars that are full of highly refined ingredients and preservatives. These buns are portable, last for several days, and really fill you up. If you must eat breakfast on the run – eat these.

Soaked muesli
150 g/1¼ cups muesli of your choice (the sugar-free kind is best and I like lots of fruit and nuts but appreciate you may not)

150 g/⅔ cup cold water

Dough
300 g/2⅓ cups wholemeal/whole-wheat or spelt flour (or a mixture)

50 g/⅓ cup dark or light rye flour

1.5 g/¾ teaspoon instant yeast, 3 g/1 teaspoon dry yeast, or 6 g/0.2 oz fresh yeast

250 g/1 cup water

6 g/1½ teaspoons salt

2–3 tablespoons molasses/dark treacle, honey or maple syrup

Decoration
muesli

prepared baking sheets (see page 9)

Makes 10 buns

Put the muesli in a little bowl, cover with the water and allow to soak for at least 1 hour before making the dough. You can leave it all day or overnight if you want.

If you are using instant or fresh yeast, put all the ingredients, excluding the soaked muesli, into a big mixing bowl and bring them together into a big ball. Turn the ball out onto the counter and knead it for a good 10 minutes. It will be sticky and that is okay.

If you are using dry yeast, put the flour into a big mixing bowl and make a well. Sprinkle in the yeast and pour in 100 g/scant ½ cup of the water. Cover and allow to rest for 15 minutes. You may or may not get a beige sludge on the top of the water, but don't worry – what is important is to dissolve the yeast. Add all the other ingredients, excluding the soaked muesli, and bring them together into a ball in the bowl. Turn the ball out onto the counter and knead it for a good 10 minutes. It will be sticky and that is okay.

Pop the kneaded dough back into the bowl, cover and allow to rest for 20 minutes. Add the soaked muesli, squishing it into the dough thoroughly. Cover again and allow to rest for 2–3 hours or overnight/all day in the fridge if you like.

Pull the very sticky dough out onto a floured surface.

Shaping
Preheat the oven to 220°C (425°F) Gas 7 before you start as these buns do not require a second rise.

Divide the dough into 10 equal portions and roll each portion into a tight ball (see page 13).

Fill a big dinner plate with muesli. Roll a ball of dough around on the plate and stretch it out at the same time to make a sausage about 10 cm/4 inches long. Place on the prepared baking sheet. Repeat with the rest of the dough, leaving some space between each bun.

Flatten the buns slightly so they are no more than about 1.5 cm/⅝ inch thick and then spray or brush liberally with water. Bake in the preheated oven for 20 minutes. Remove from the oven and allow to cool on a wire rack before eating.

Laugenbrötchen German-Speaking Area

Laugen literally means 'lye' in German and laugenbrot is a catch-all for bread that is simmered briefly in a vat of lye water before it is baked. The simmering gives the bread its distinctive colour, texture and flavour. Fear not, however! You can achieve the same thing with a simple simmering solution of bicarbonate of soda/baking soda and water. This style of bun is found all over southern Germany, Austria and Switzerland.

Predough
50 g/⅓ cup strong white (bread) flour
50 g/3½ tablespoons water
pinch of yeast (any kind will do)

Dough
500 g/3¾ cups strong white (bread) flour
2.5 g/1¼ teaspoons instant yeast, 5 g/1¾ teaspoons dry yeast, or 10 g/0.35 oz fresh yeast
150 g/⅔ cup water
150 g/⅔ cup milk (straight from the fridge is fine)
10 g/2½ teaspoons salt
50 g/3 tablespoons lard (you can substitute butter)

For the simmering bath
1 litre/4 cups water
4 tablespoons/¼ cup bicarbonate of soda/baking soda

Decoration
coarse salt, to sprinkle

large saucepan
prepared baking sheets (see page 9)

Makes 16 buns

Day One: making a predough
Put all the ingredients for the predough in a big bowl and give them a good stir. Cover with clingfilm/plastic wrap and leave overnight on the counter.

Day Two: making the dough
Put the flour into a big mixing bowl and make a well. Sprinkle the yeast in the well and pour over the water. Flick some flour on the water to close the well. Cover and allow to rest for 1 hour. Add the remaining ingredients including the predough and mix them together in the bowl. Turn the dough out onto the counter and knead it well for 10 minutes. Pop it back in the bowl, cover and allow to rest for 2 hours.

Scrape the dough out gently onto an unfloured surface.

Shaping (little submarines)
Divide the dough into 4 equal portions. Shape each portion into a tight sausage (see page 11). Divide each sausage into a further 4 portions and allow to rest for 15 minutes under a dry tea towel. Shape each portion into a tight ball (see page 12) and allow to rest for 5 minutes. Using your hands, roll each ball out into a little submarine shape and allow to rest under a dry tea towel for 45 minutes.

(Continued overleaf.)

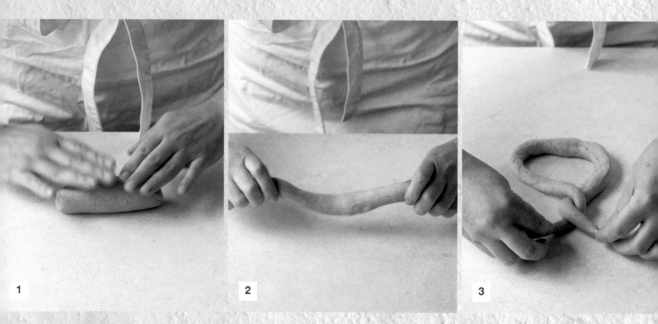

1

2

3

Shaping (pretzels, knots and sticks)

Divide the dough into 4 equal portions and shape each portion into a tight sausage (see page 11). [1]

And now it is really up to you. If you want big fat squashy pretzels or buns, divide each sausage into 4 pieces. You will have 16 big pretzels or buns. If you want small, dainty, more crispy pretzels or buns, divide each sausage into 8 pieces. You will have 32 smaller pretzels or buns. If you want teeny tiny crispy pretzels or sticks – the dry kind that you buy in the snack aisle – divide the dough into little balls the size of peas.

Pop your pieces of dough on a lightly floured surface, lightly flour the tops as well, and cover them with a dry tea towel. Allow to rest for 15 minutes.

Shape each piece of dough into a tight ball (see page 12) and allow to rest under the tea towel again for 5 minutes. (If you are making the teeny tiny pea-sized pretzel sticks you can skip this step.)

For a pretzel, roll a snake about 25 cm/10 inches long. [2] Twist the head and tail ends together twice and make a circle out of the middle of the snake. [3]

Fold the twisted ends over into the middle of the circle and gently lay them down. [4, 5]

To make knots, roll each ball into a thin snake about 15 cm/6 inches long and tie a knot in the dough.

If you are making small crispy sticks, roll pea-sized balls of dough out into matchstick-sized sticks.

Place the shaped dough pieces on a floured surface and lightly flour the tops. [6] Cover them with a dry tea towel. Allow to rest for 45 minutes.

5

6

Preheat the oven to 220°C (425°F) Gas 7.

Pour the water for the simmering bath into a large saucepan. Add the bicarbonate of soda/baking soda and bring it to a boil. It does not need to be a deep pan – a wide one is better as you can fit more in at a time. Turn the heat down so that the water is simmering. Pick up each piece of dough and gently place it upside-down in the water. Don't worry about putting the tiny sticks in upside-down if that is what you are making – it's way too fiddly – just pop them in and splash them with water so they are all covered.

Fit as many as you can into the pan. Allow enough space between each shape so they don't stick together and so you can get a slotted spoon in there to fish them out easily. Leave them in the water for 20–30 seconds and then remove with the slotted spoon. The longer they are in the darker they will be when they bake.

Place the shapes right-side-up on a prepared baking sheet. They can be close together because they won't spread out in the oven, but don't let them touch. If you are making submarine-shaped buns, you can snip the tops with scissors – make 2–3 cuts, each at a 45° angle. This is purely for decoration as you will see when you bake them (the outside becomes red-brown, the inside is white).

Sprinkle with coarse salt. Fill the prepared baking sheet and then pop it in the preheated oven. Bake the buns for 15–20 minutes depending on their size. Teeny tiny ones will take 5–7 minutes only. Remove from the oven and allow to cool completely on a wire rack.

Predough
300 g/2⅓ cups plain/all-purpose
  white wheat flour
200 g/¾ cup plus 1 tablespoon
  water
pinch of yeast (any kind will do)

Dough
125 g/½ cup water
1.25 g/¾ teaspoon instant yeast,
  2.5 g/1 teaspoon dry yeast, or
  5 g/0.17 oz fresh yeast
250 g/2 cups plain/all-purpose
  white wheat flour
5 g/1¼ teaspoons salt

prepared baking sheets (see page 9)

Makes 16 buns

Spaccatini Italy

This is a lovely, plain white bun from Italy. The things that make it special are its flavour and its distinctive bottom-like shape. The buns take time to rise and, as they do, the flavour develops.

Day One: making a predough
Put the ingredients in a bowl and mix with your hands. There is no need to knead it. Cover with clingfilm/plastic wrap and leave on the counter for 24–48 hours. The longer you leave it the stronger the flavour will be.

Day Two: making the dough
Pour the water over the predough and, using your hands, make a milky paste. Add the yeast and allow to rest for 15 minutes. Add the flour and the salt and bring the ingredients together in a big ball. Turn the dough out and knead it well for 10 minutes. This is a stiff dough.

Pop it back in the bowl, cover and allow to rest for 2 hours.

Pull the dough out gently onto an unfloured surface.

Shaping
Divide the dough into 16 equal portions. Shape each portion into a tight ball (see page 12) and, using the round edge of a metal skewer or a chopstick, press firmly down across each bun to make a deep cleft – right to the bottom. [1] Place the buns cleft-side-down on a floury surface and cover with a dry tea towel. Allow to rest for 1 hour.

Preheat the oven to 220°C (425°F) Gas 7.

Turn each bun over and place them cleft-side-up on the prepared baking sheet. Using a razor or a knife, open up the clefts if they have closed whilst rising. [2]

Pop the buns in the preheated oven to bake for 20 minutes. Remove from the oven and allow to cool completely on a wire rack. Enjoy them with salad, soup or a simple pasta dish.

Bastounakia Greece

These are delicious, chewy buns and are perfect for casual meals, picnics and lunchboxes. They are a bit of a cross between an Italian breadstick and a French baguette. Simple and fun to make, you can personalize them by filling them with anything you like.

Predough
100 g/scant ½ cup warm water
150 g/1 generous cup plain/all-purpose white wheat flour
pinch of yeast (any kind will do)

Dough
1.5g/¾ teaspoon instant yeast, 3 g/1 teaspoon dry yeast, or 6 g/0.2 oz fresh yeast
250 g/1 cup water
300 g/2⅓ cups plain/all-purpose white wheat flour
(Note: there is no salt in the dough)

Filling
olive oil
8–10 g/2–2½ teaspoons coarse sea salt, depending on how much you like salt
the needles from 4 big sprigs of fresh rosemary (or any other herb you like)

prepared baking sheets (see page 9)

Makes 16 sticks

Day One: making a predough

Mix together the water, flour and yeast until they are well blended. Cover with clingfilm/plastic wrap and allow to rest on the counter for 12–48 hours. The longer the predough rests, the stronger the buns will taste.

Day Two: making the dough

If you are using instant or fresh yeast, put all the ingredients including the predough into a bowl. Gather the ingredients together into a ball. Pull out onto the counter and knead well for 10 minutes. It will be sticky.

If you are using dry yeast, put the flour into a bowl and make a well. Add 100 g/scant ½ cup of the water and allow to rest for 15 minutes. A beige sludge may or may not appear on the top of the dough. Don't worry – as long as the yeast is dissolved it will be fine. Add the rest of the water and the predough and gather the ingredients together into a ball. Pull out onto the counter and knead well for 10 minutes. It will be sticky.

Flour a surface on which you can cut (this will become clear later). Stretch out the dough to a thickness of about 5 mm/¼ inch. Brush the top with olive oil and cover it with clingfilm/plastic wrap. Allow to rest for 1 hour.

(Continued overleaf.)

My friend Kathy comes from Greece and she remembers her grandmother and all of her aunts preparing bread 'by eye'. They never measured anything, just popped the ingredients into a big bowl and kneaded away. They baked their bread in an oven her grandfather built in the bottom of the garden. It's the best thing she ever remembers eating. And she is a trained chef.

Shaping

Remove the clingfilm/plastic wrap. Scatter a third of the salt and rosemary over the dough. [1] Fold the top edge of the dough to the middle [2] and fold the bottom edge in over the top as if you were folding a piece of paper into thirds for an envelope. [3]

Turn the dough ¼ of a turn and roll the dough flat again. [4] Brush some more olive oil on the dough and scatter another third of the salt and rosemary on the top. Fold, turn and roll the dough flat once more, brush some more olive oil on it and scatter the final third of the salt and rosemary over the dough. Fold the dough one last time, lightly flour it and flip it over so the floury side is down. Flour the top and cover it with a dry tea towel and allow to rest for 45 minutes.

Preheat the oven to 230°C (450°F) Gas 8.

Using a knife, scraper or pizza cutter, cut the dough into strips about 2.5 cm/1 inch wide. [5] If the strips are too long, cut them in half. [6]

Place the strips on the prepared baking sheet and brush them with olive oil. Sprinkle them with more salt if you would like to. Pop them in the preheated oven for 20 minutes. Remove from the oven and brush with olive oil while they are still hot. [7] Transfer to a wire rack. It is hard to resist eating these warm!

5

6

7

Kahvalti Turkey

Kahvalti simply means 'breakfast' in Turkish and there are many kinds of breakfast buns in Turkey, including Pide Ekmeghi and Simit the recipes for which you can find in my first book. I came across Kahvalti about a million years ago when I was back-packing through Turkey. My friend Sheila and I stayed with a gorgeous family in Bodrum. The father ran a coffee shop and the mother baked like a pro. Every day she would prepare a Turkish breakfast (eggs, honey, yogurt, cheese, coffee...) with a different kind of bread. We loved this one the best.

350 g/2¾ cups strong white (bread) flour

2 g/1 teaspoon instant yeast, 3.5 g/1⅛ teaspoons dry yeast, or 7 g/0.25 oz fresh yeast

240 g/1 cup milk, heated up to just below boiling point, then cooled to room temperature

5 g/1¼ teaspoons salt

1 medium potato, peeled, cooked and mashed (and cooled)

100 g/3½ oz crumbled feta cheese

Glaze
1 egg white
1 teaspoon water

Decoration
nigella seeds (or black sesame seeds, or poppy seeds if you cannot get either)

prepared baking sheets (see page 9)

Makes 12 buns

Put the flour into a big bowl and make a well. Sprinkle the yeast in the well and pour over the milk. Flick flour over the well to close it and allow to rest for 1 hour.

Put all the other ingredients except the cheese into the bowl and mix together in a big ball. Turn it out onto the counter and knead well for 10 minutes. It will be a bit sticky but don't add more flour. Pop it back into the bowl and allow to rest for 20 minutes or so. Mix in the cheese (you can do this right in the bowl), gently squashing the dough around the cheese so that you have some yummy big cheesy bits in the final buns. Don't worry about the dough, it will recover. Form the dough back into a ball, cover and allow to rest for 2 hours.

Pull the dough gently out onto a floured surface.

Shaping

Shape the dough into a tight sausage (see page 11). Divide the dough into 12 equal portions, dust with flour, cover with a dry tea towel and allow to rest for 15 minutes.

Flour your hands and shape each little portion of dough into a tight ball (see page 13). Pop the balls on the prepared baking sheet, cover with a dry tea towel and allow to rest for 1 hour.

Preheat the oven to 220°C (425°F) Gas 7.

Mix together the egg white and water for the glaze and brush the buns with the glaze. Sprinkle with the nigella seeds before popping them in the preheated oven and baking them for 20 minutes. Remove from the oven and transfer to a wire rack. Try to wait for them to cool before breaking into them or you will burn your greedy tongue on melty cheese!

Pirozhki Eastern Europe

These stuffed buns are fried rather than baked. They are found all over Eastern Europe, Central Asia and into Greece and come in many different forms. You can stuff them with whatever you like and the suggestion here is typically Polish – potatoes, onions and dill. It is a delicious combination and, when combined with meat or fish, makes an elegant meal. Alternatively serve them with soup or salad, take them on a picnic or pack them in a lunchbox.

250 g/1 cup milk, heated up to just below boiling point, then cooled to room temperature
500 g/4 cups plain/all-purpose white wheat flour
2.5 g/1¼ teaspoons instant yeast, 5 g/1¾ teaspoons dry yeast, or 10 g/0.35 oz fresh yeast
2 eggs
50 g/3 tablespoons unsalted butter, melted and cooled
10 g/2½ teaspoons salt

Filling
4 potatoes, peeled
2 onions, diced
2 tablespoons butter or lard
1 tablespoon fresh dill, chopped
salt and pepper

To fry
clarified butter, lard or good quality oil with a high smoke point

heavy-based frying pan

Makes 25–30 buns

For the filling, cook the potatoes in plenty of boiling water, drain and cut into small cubes. Sweat the onions for a good 10 minutes in the butter or lard (on a low heat with the lid on) and then add the potatoes, dill and salt and pepper to taste. Stir the potatoes around, turn the heat off and cover the saucepan. Set aside.

Put the flour into a big bowl and make a well. Sprinkle the yeast into the well, then add the milk. Flick flour over the milk to close the well. Cover and allow to rest for 1 hour. Mix in all the other ingredients and gather into a big ball. Turn the dough out onto the counter and knead well for 10 minutes.

Pop the dough back in the bowl. Cover and allow to rest for 2 hours.

Pull the dough out of the bowl onto a floured surface.

Shaping
Have a little bowl of water to hand to brush the pirozhki dough with water.

Divide the dough into portions about the size of ping pong balls. Take one of the portions and, using a rolling pin, roll it out into a circle (an oval will do). Brush the edge of the dough with water and pop a little spoonful of the filling into the middle. Fold the disc in half to make a half-moon shaped parcel and seal the edges (see page 15 'to fill and shape an oblong'). Place seam-side-down on a lightly floured surface and cover with a dry tea towel. Repeat until you have used all the little balls of dough and the filling. Allow to rest for 45 minutes.

Heat the fat in a heavy-based frying pan and put in some pirozhkis. Give them space to cook evenly and give yourself space to flip them. Fry them on a low heat for about 10 minutes in total, flipping frequently so they don't burn. Transfer to a plate lined with kitchen paper/paper towels to drain.

Bublik Eastern Europe

Bublik are eaten all over Eastern Europe and Russia. Although they look like bagels (or bagels look like them), bublik are not breakfast food. They are sweeter than bagels and are typically eaten with a cup of tea or coffee in the middle of the morning. If you are travelling in the rural parts of these lovely lands you may still see them for sale by the dozen and strung on a string.

400 g/3 cups strong white (bread) flour
3 tablespoons sugar
2 g/1 teaspoon instant yeast, 4 g/1¼ teaspoons dry yeast, or 8 g/0.28 oz fresh yeast
250 g/1 cup milk, heated up to just below boiling point, then cooled to room temperature
8 g/2 teaspoons salt
50 g/3 tablespoons butter

For the simmering bath
water

Glaze
1 egg, beaten
1 teaspoon water

Decoration
poppy seeds

prepared baking sheets (see page 9)

Makes 12 buns

Put the flour into a bowl and make a well. Sprinkle the sugar and yeast into the well and pour over the milk. Close the well by flicking flour on the surface of the milk. Cover and allow to rest for 1 hour.

Add the rest of the ingredients and bring the dough together into a ball in a bowl. Turn out onto the counter and knead well for 10 minutes. Return it to the bowl and allow to rest for 2 hours, covered with clingfilm/plastic wrap or a damp tea towel.

Gently pull the dough out onto a floured surface.

Shaping
Shape the dough into a tight sausage (see page 11) and divide it into 12 equal portions. Allow to rest for 15 minutes under a dry tea towel.

Shape each portion into a tight ball (see page 12). Allow to rest under a dry tea towel for 15 minutes.

Poke a hole in each ball with the round end of a wooden spoon or a chopstick that you have covered in flour and then stretch out each piece so that it is a circle. Make the hole at least 4 cm/1½ inches in diameter otherwise they will close up completely while they rise. Do this for all the pieces and allow to rest for 30 minutes under a dry tea towel on a floured surface.

Pour the water for the simmering bath into a large saucepan. Bring the water to a simmer.

Preheat the oven to 220°C (425°F) Gas 7.

Stretch the bubliks out again so the holes are pronounced and place each one into the water for 30 seconds. Fit in as many as you can comfortably get into the saucepan. Lift them out and place them on the prepared baking sheet. Combine the egg and the water for the glaze. Glaze each bublik and sprinkle with the poppy seeds.

Pop them in the preheated oven and bake for 20–25 minutes. Remove from the oven and allow to cool completely on a wire rack.

Piragi Estonia

Years ago I joined my friend, Elizabeth, on a trip to Estonia. Over one snowy weekend we delighted in a charming, walled city, and stuffed ourselves with all sorts of Baltic baked goods including these buns stuffed with smoked pork.

450 g/3⅔ cups plain/all-purpose white wheat flour

2 g/1⅛ teaspoons instant yeast, 4.5 g/1½ teaspoons dry yeast, or 9 g/0.3 oz fresh yeast

200 g/¾ cup plus 1 tablespoon milk heated up to just below boiling point, then cooled to room temperature

50 g/3 tablespoons butter, melted and allowed to cool

30 g/2 tablespoons sour cream

9 g/2¼ teaspoons salt

Filling

300 g/10½ oz bacon (or country ham, pancetta, speck, or lardons)

1 onion, finely diced

Glaze

1 egg, beaten

1 teaspoon water

pinch of salt

prepared baking sheets (see page 9)

Makes 20–24 buns

Put the flour into a big bowl and make a well. Sprinkle the yeast into the well and pour over the milk. Flick flour over the milk to close the well, cover and allow to rest for 1 hour. Add the rest of the dough ingredients and bring them together into a big ball in the bowl and then turn the dough out onto the counter. Knead well for 10 minutes.

Put the kneaded dough back in the bowl. Cover and allow to rest for 2 hours.

While the dough is resting, make the filling. Fry the bacon in a frying pan for 5 minutes on a medium heat. Then add the onion and fry on a low heat for 10 minutes until the onion is transparent. Remove this from the pan with a slotted spoon and place on paper towels/kitchen paper to drain and cool down.

Pull the dough out onto a lightly floured surface.

Shaping

Have a little bowl of water handy as you will need it to brush each piragi with water before you seal it.

Divide the dough into little balls each about the size of a ping pong ball.

Using a rolling pin, roll each little ball into a small disc and brush water all around the edge. Place a little blob of the filling in the centre of each little disc and then bring the edges of the dough up around the filling, making a half moon. Then, starting from the seam, roll them up as tightly as you can. Pinch the ends so they are pointy and place them seam-side-down on the prepared baking sheet (see page 15 'to fill and shape an oblong'). Lightly flour them and cover with a dry tea towel. Allow to rest for 45 minutes.

Preheat the oven to 220°C (425°F) Gas 7.

For the glaze, mix together the egg, water and salt and brush over the piragi. Pop them in the preheated oven for 15 minutes. They will be golden brown when they are done. Remove from the oven and transfer to a wire rack. Serve them with sour cream as a pre-dinner nibble, as part of a light meal or on picnics and in lunchboxes.

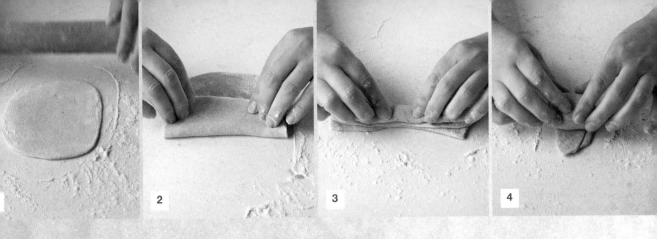

2   3   4

Meloui   Morocco

When my friend Erlend turned 40 he celebrated by inviting friends to stay in a little house on a beach in Morocco. We were amazed by the quality and the variety of the bread. We had meloui for breakfast with a spread of half honey and half butter. You cannot imagine how good they were!

250 g/2 cups strong white (bread) flour
3 g/1½ teaspoons instant yeast, 6 g/2 teaspoons dry yeast, or 12 g/ 0.42 oz fresh yeast
375 g/1½ cups water
350 g/2⅔ cups semolina
12 g/1 tablespoon salt

Filling
250 g/1 cup melted clarified butter or ghee (cooled slightly) or good quality olive oil
100 g/¾ cup semolina

a large frying pan
prepared baking sheets (see page 9)

Makes 20 little buns

If you are using instant or fresh yeast, put all the ingredients into a bowl and bring them together into a ball. Pull the dough out onto the counter and knead well for 10 minutes.

If you are using dry yeast, put the flour into a bowl and make a well. Sprinkle the yeast into the well, pour the water over it and allow to rest for 15 minutes. A beige sludge may or may not form on top of the water – don't worry about it, the thing is to let the yeast dissolve thoroughly. Add the rest of the ingredients and bring them into a ball. Pull the dough out onto the counter and knead well for 10 minutes.

Pop it back into the bowl, cover and allow to rest for 1–2 hours.

Pull the dough gently out onto an unfloured surface.

Shaping

Divide the dough into 20 equal portions and shape each portion into a tight ball (see page 12). Allow to rest for 15 minutes under a dry tea towel.

Take a ball and, on a floury surface, roll it with a rolling pin as thinly as you can into a square. [1] Brush the dough with melted butter or oil and sprinkle semolina on it.

Fold the dough into thirds as you would fold a piece of paper for an envelope. Gently pull on the corners as you fold so that they reach the edges evenly. [2]

Brush the dough again with melted butter or oil and sprinkle with semolina. Fold it again as above or roll it up so that you have a thin strip. [3] Roll it gently with a rolling pin into a long, thin strip that is about 2.5 cm/1 inch wide. Brush the top of the strip with melted butter or oil and roll it up from a short end so that it resembles a snail shell. [4] Pinch the edge slightly into the main part of the bun so it does not unravel. Brush the top and bottom with melted butter or oil. Repeat with the remaining balls.

Heat the remaining butter or oil in a large frying pan. Flatten the buns to a thickness of 1 cm/½ inch and fry for 8–10 minutes, flipping them regularly so they don't burn. Drain them on kitchen paper/paper towels before eating.

Khubza Bil Ashab Libya

Libya is 90% desert and is not a wheat-growing nation. However, like its North African and Middle Eastern neighbours, Libya has been trading wheat with countries around the Mediterranean and in the fertile crescent since the beginning of, well, wheat! The bread in Libya, like the bread in the rest of the region, is delicious. This herb bread is really simple because it requires no kneading at all. It is perfect every time and is eaten in Libya as a late-night snack, accompanied by tea and lots of chatter. It is perfect as a finger food at parties and picnics and will be a winner in any lunchbox.

600 g/4½ cups strong white or wholemeal/whole-wheat (bread) flour (or a mixture)

3 g/1½ teaspoons instant yeast, 6 g/2 teaspoons dry yeast, or 12 g/0.42 oz fresh yeast

12 g/1 tablespoon salt (unless you are adding olives, in which case cut it down to 8 g/2 teaspoons)

50 g/3 tablespoons olive oil

500 g/2 cups water

any combination of: diced olives, chopped spring onions/scallions or red onions, crumbled feta cheese, a few handfuls of fresh herbs (such as marjoram, chives, parsley), pinch of paprika, zahtar or other spices

prepared baking sheets (see page 9)

Makes 16 buns

Day One: making the dough
The night before you would like your bread, put everything into a big mixing bowl and stir well. Cover with clingfilm/plastic wrap and pop it in the fridge. Allow to rest until the next day.

Day Two: shaping
Preheat the oven to 220°C (425°F) Gas 7.

Take the dough out of the fridge and gently pull it out onto a floured surface.

Divide the dough into 16 equal portions and then, with floury hands, shape into balls (see page 13). Transfer to the prepared baking sheet.

Pop them immediately in the preheated oven and bake for 20 minutes. Remove from the oven and allow to cool completely on a wire rack.

Predough

150 g/1 generous cup
  strong white or wholemeal/
  whole-wheat (bread) flour
125 g/½ cup water
pinch of yeast (any kind will do)

Dough

150 g/1 generous cup
  strong white or wholemeal/
  whole-wheat (bread) flour
2 g/1 teaspoon instant yeast,
  4 g/1¼ teaspoons dry yeast,
  or 8 g/0.28 oz fresh yeast
250 g/1 cup water
225 g/1⅔ cups finely ground
  semolina
10 g/2½ teaspoons salt
30 g/2 tablespoons olive oil
1 tablespoon mixed whole spice
  seeds, such as anise, cumin,
  sesame, celery etc

Decoration

1 tablespoon mixed whole spice
  seeds (as above)

prepared baking sheets (see page 9)

Makes 12 buns

1

Khubz Mbassis Tunisia

This recipe comes from Tunisia where many people still take their dough to the bakery to be baked in the communal oven. Do feel free to vary the spices and seeds but don't omit the semolina as it gives the bread a distinctive texture.

Day One: making a predough

Put the ingredients for the predough into a big bowl and give them a good stir. Cover and leave overnight on the counter.

Day Two: making the dough

Put the flour into a big mixing bowl. Make a well in the flour and sprinkle in the yeast. Pour over half of the water and allow to rest for 15 minutes or so. Pour in the rest of the water, add all the other ingredients including the predough and mix them together in the bowl. Turn the dough out onto the counter and knead it well for 10 minutes. Pop it back in the bowl, cover and allow to rest for 1–2 hours.

Gently pull the dough out onto an unfloured surface.

Shaping

Shape the dough into a tight sausage (see page 11). Divide the sausage into 12 equal portions and pop them on a lightly floured surface. Cover with a dry tea towel and allow to rest for 15 minutes.

Shape each portion into a tight ball (see page 12). Pop all the balls back on the lightly floured surface and cover them with a dry tea towel. Allow to rest for 5 minutes.

Lightly flour part of the counter and take one of the balls of dough. Using your hands, gently stretch it into a disc about 6 cm/2½ inches in diameter. Using your thumb or fingertip, press firmly down at the edge of the disc, making an indentation at the edge of the dough. Do this all the way around the disc, leaving 1 cm/½ inch or so between each indentation. [1]

Pick up the shaped bun with a scraper and pop it on the prepared baking sheet. Do this for all the buns, making sure there is a bit of space between them. Cover the buns with a dry tea towel and allow to rest for 45 minutes.

Preheat the oven to 220°C (425°F) Gas 7.

Before you bake the buns, brush them with water and sprinkle the seeds on the top. Push down the dimpled edges again so that the indentations stay while the buns bake. Pop them in the preheated oven and bake for 20 minutes. Remove from the oven and allow them to cool on a wire rack.

Sfoof Lebanon

In London, where I live, there are plenty of excellent Lebanese shops and restaurants and both sell a tempting array of sweet things. Among the different kinds of baklava there are usually some other baked goodies including Sfoofs. The name says it all, really, and of course they are great. The turmeric makes them eye catching and the spices and nuts make them delicious.

500 g/4 cups plain/
    all-purpose white
    wheat flour
2.5 g/1¼ teaspoons
    instant yeast, 5 g/1¾
    teaspoons dry yeast, or
    10 g/0.35 oz fresh yeast
80 g/scant ½ cup sugar
250 g/1 cup milk, heated
    to just below boiling
    point and cooled to
    room temperature
12 g/1 tablespoon salt
2 eggs
1 tablespoon anise seeds
2 teaspoons ground
    turmeric
1 teaspoon ground
    mahlab (or 1 teaspoon
    of the following mixture:
    1½ teaspoons ground
    cinnamon, ¼ teaspoon
    ground cloves,
    ¼ teaspoon ground bay
    leaves)
1 teaspoon orange
    blossom water
100 g/6½ tablespoons
    butter

Glaze
1 egg, beaten
1 tablespoon water
pinch of salt
pinch of sugar

Decoration
pistachios

*prepared baking sheets
  (see page 9)*

Makes 12 buns

Put the flour into a bowl and make a well. Sprinkle the yeast and the sugar into the well and pour over the milk. Flick some flour on top of the milk to close the well. Cover and allow to rest for 1 hour.

While you wait, chop the pistachios for decoration by hand into coarse bits.

When the dough has rested, sprinkle the salt around the edge of the flour and add the eggs, spices and orange blossom water into the middle of the dough. Bring the ingredients together into a ball in the bowl and then tip this out onto the counter.

Knead for 10 minutes and then add the butter bit by bit. Knead for another 10–15 minutes until the butter is well integrated and the dough is deep yellow and shiny. The dough will be sticky and that is fine. Don't be tempted to add more flour.

Pop the dough back in the bowl, cover and allow to rest for 2 hours.

Pull the dough gently out onto a floured surface.

(Continued overleaf.)

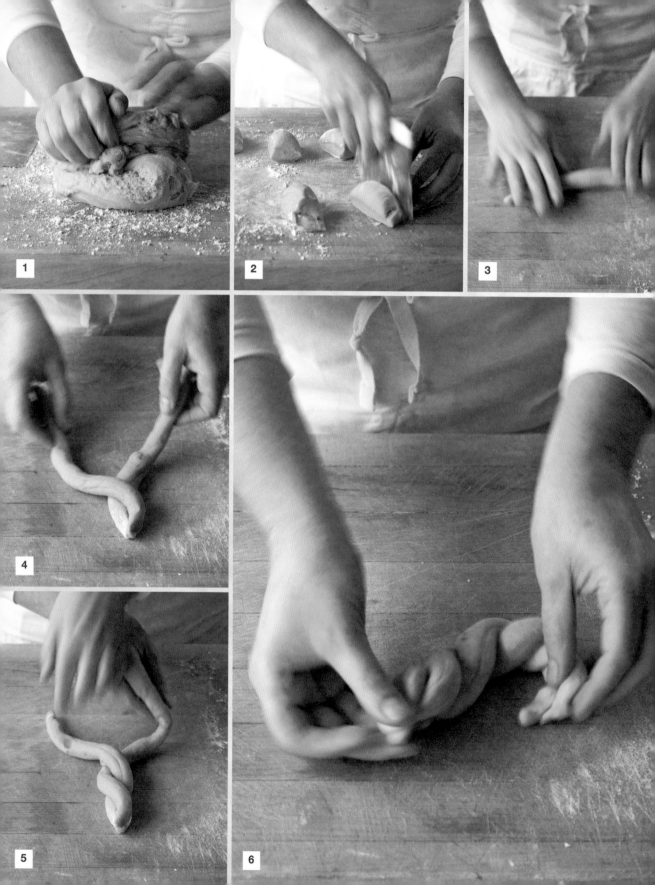

Shaping

Shape the dough into a tight sausage (see page 11).
[1] Divide the dough into 24 equal portions. [2]
Roll each portion into a long thin rope about 20 cm/
8 inches long. [3]

Take 2 ropes and twist them together. [4, 5]

Form the twisted ropes into a ring and pinch the
ends to seal it shut. [6, 7]

Repeat with the remaining dough until you have
12 twisty rings.

Place the rings on the prepared baking sheet. [8]
Cover with a dry tea towel and allow to rest for 1 hour.

Preheat the oven to 220°C (425°F) Gas 7.

To make the glaze, mix together the beaten egg,
water, salt and sugar. Brush each bun with the glaze.
Sprinkle the buns with the chopped pistachios.

Pop the buns in the preheated oven and bake for
15 minutes. Remove from the oven and allow to cool
completely on a wire rack.

Khubz Mahala Iran

This bread is eaten any time of day. Its slight sweetness lends itself to breakfast but then again, it is really nice at lunch or dinner with traditional Middle Eastern treats such as hummus, minced lamb, or seasoned yogurt. A glass of hot tea to round it off and you have a meal fit for a king.

200 g/1⅓ cups pitted
   dates, dried or fresh
700 g/5⅔ cups plain/
   all-purpose white or
   wholemeal/whole-wheat
   wheat flour
3.5 g/1¾ teaspoons
   instant yeast, 7 g/2¼
   teaspoons dry yeast, or
   14 g/0.5 oz fresh yeast
200 g/¾ cup plus
   1 tablespoon water
10 g/2½ teaspoons salt
4 teaspoons rose water or
   orange blossom water

Glaze
1 egg, beaten
1 tablespoon water
pinch of salt
pinch of sugar

Decoration
sesame seeds

*prepared baking sheets
  (see page 9)*

Makes 20 buns

Put the dates into a small saucepan and just cover them with water. Cover the pan and simmer the dates for 30 minutes or so, until they are very soft. Mush this mixture (put it in a blender or push it through a sieve/strainer) and allow to cool completely.

If you are using instant or fresh yeast, put all the ingredients including the cooked dates into a big bowl and bring them together. Turn the dough out onto the counter and knead for 10 minutes. This dough is really sticky but don't be tempted to add more flour.

If you are using dry yeast, put the flour into a big bowl and make a well in it. Sprinkle the yeast into the well and add 100 g/scant ½ cup of the water. Cover with a dry tea towel and allow to rest for 15 minutes. A beige sludge may or may not appear on the top of the water and that is fine, as long as the yeast is fully dissolved. After 15 minutes add all the other ingredients including the cooked dates and bring them together in a ball in the bowl. Turn the ball out on the counter and knead for 10 minutes. This dough is really sticky but don't be tempted to add more flour.

Pop the dough back in the bowl, cover and allow to rest for 1–2 hours.

Pull the dough out onto a well floured surface.

Shaping
Divide the dough into 20 equal portions, lightly flour the tops, and allow to rest under a dry tea towel for 15 minutes.

Shape each portion into a tight ball (see page 13) and allow to rest again for 5–10 minutes. The dough is soft but you want to resist adding any more flour. If you are sticking to the dough, flour your hands lightly.

Take a ball of dough and gently flatten it with a rolling pin until it is a disc about 5 mm/¼ inch thick. Place on a prepared baking sheet. Repeat for all the balls. Cover again with a dry tea towel and allow to rest for 45 minutes.

Preheat the oven to 220°C (425°F) Gas 7.

Beat together the ingredients for the glaze and brush the buns with the glaze. Dimple the buns with your fingertips and sprinkle sesame seeds on top. Pop them in the preheated oven for 15 minutes. Remove from the oven. Wrap the buns up in a cloth to keep them soft. These are best eaten the moment they are baked but they keep pretty well too.

Bun Muska Iran

These little buns resemble hamburger buns but fret not! They are much more delicious than the average hamburger bun because they are enriched with eggs, butter, milk and just a little bit of sugar. Wherever there is a Persian community you will find them being consumed with copious amounts of butter on top, and accompanied by cups of sweet, milky tea.

350 g/2¾ cups plain/all-purpose white wheat flour
2 g/1 teaspoon instant yeast, 4 g/1¼ teaspoons dry yeast, or 8 g/0.28 oz fresh yeast
50 g/¼ cup sugar
150 g/⅔ cup milk, heated up to just below boiling point, then cooled to room temperature
8 g/2 teaspoons salt
1 egg
50 g/3 tablespoons butter, cubed, at room temperature

Glaze
1 egg, beaten
1 tablespoon water
pinch of salt
pinch of sugar

Decoration
mixed sesame seeds

prepared baking sheets (see page 9)

Makes 8 buns

Put the flour into a big mixing bowl and make a well in it. Sprinkle in the yeast and the sugar and then pour over the cooled milk. Flick flour over the well to close it and cover. Allow to rest for 1 hour.

After it has rested, add the salt and the egg and bring the ingredients together in the bowl. Turn the dough out onto the counter and knead it well for 10 minutes. Then add the butter and knead for another 10 minutes. Put the dough back in the bowl, cover and allow to rest for 2 hours.

Gently pull the dough out onto an unfloured surface.

Shaping
Divide the dough into 8 equal portions and shape them into tight balls (see page 12).

Place the balls on the prepared baking sheet. Cover with a dry tea towel and allow to rest for 45 minutes.

Preheat the oven to 220°C (425°F) Gas 7.

Beat the ingredients for the glaze together and brush each bun liberally with it. Sprinkle the sesame seeds on top and pop them in the preheated oven. Bake for 20 minutes.

Remove from the oven and cool completely on a wire rack. Eat with lashings of butter and hot, sweet, milky tea.

Ka'ak Syria

Although this particular recipe comes from a Syrian friend, Ka'ak are eaten all over the Fertile Crescent. If you like crunchy, these are for you! The key ingredient is a spice called 'mahlab', which is the stone from the St Lucie cherry. You can buy it in Greek, Turkish and Middle Eastern shops and you can get it either whole (and grind it at home) or ground.

450 g/3¼ cups strong white (bread) flour
2 g/1⅛ teaspoons instant yeast, 4.5 g/1½ teaspoons dry yeast, or 9 g/0.3 oz fresh yeast
250 g/1 cup water
9 g/2¼ teaspoons salt
50 g/3 tablespoons butter or good quality olive oil
1 teaspoon ground cumin
1 teaspoon ground mahlab (see page 49)
1 teaspoon ground kizabrah (or ground anise)

Decoration
1 egg, beaten with 1 teaspoon water
sesame seeds

prepared baking sheets (see page 9)

Makes 30–50 buns

If you are using instant or fresh yeast, put all the ingredients into a bowl and bring them together into a ball. Turn the dough ball out of the bowl onto the counter and knead well for 10 minutes.

If you are using dry yeast, put the flour into a bowl and make a well in it. Sprinkle the yeast into the well, pour over 100 g/scant ½ cup of the water, then allow to rest for 15 minutes. You may or may not get a beige sludge on the top of the water, but don't worry – what is important is to dissolve the yeast. Add the rest of the ingredients and bring them into a ball in the bowl. Turn the dough ball out of the bowl onto the counter and knead well for 10 minutes.

Pop the dough back into the bowl, cover and allow to rest for 2 hours.

Pull the dough out gently onto an unfloured surface.

Shaping

Preheat the oven to 230°C (450°F) Gas 8 before you start as these buns do not require a second rise.

Divide the dough into little portions about the size of a walnut. Roll each portion into a thin snake about 10 cm/4 inches long. Form the snake into a circle and seal the ends together by pinching tightly.

Dip each circle into a shallow bowl of the beaten egg mixture and then into the sesame seeds. Place each circle on a prepared baking sheet.

When the sheet is full, pop it immediately in the preheated oven and bake the buns for 10 minutes. Turn the oven down to 180°C (350°F) Gas 4 and bake the buns for a further 15 minutes. Remove from the oven and allow to cool completely on a wire rack.

Bake all the buns in this way and if you find they are not completely dry when they have cooled – if there is any squish in them at all – pile them all back on a baking sheet and put them in the oven. Turn the oven to its lowest setting and leave them there for several hours (or overnight) until they are totally dry. That way, they last for weeks in an airtight container.

Char Sui Bao China

If you have ever eaten Dim Sum, you have probably eaten Char Sui Bao. These are lovely fluffy white buns that are stuffed with barbecued pork. In the West we tend to see them only on the Dim Sum menu but in Asia they are a popular snack and you see them everywhere – in little shops and on the street where they are sold from steamy hand carts.

185 g/¾ cup water
30 g/2 tablespoons plus
   1 teaspoon sugar
300 g/2⅓ cups plain/
   all-purpose white
   wheat flour
1.5 g/¾ teaspoon instant
   yeast, 3 g/1 teaspoon
   dry yeast, or 6 g/0.2 oz
   fresh yeast
1 tablespoon lard or
   neutral vegetable oil

For the shaping
½ teaspoon baking
   powder
sesame oil

Filling
1 tablespoon melted lard
   or neutral vegetable oil
1 spring onion/scallion,
   finely chopped
1 garlic clove, minced
125 g/4 oz barbecued
   pork, cut into small
   cubes (you can
   substitute chicken, fish,
   tofu or mushrooms)
1 tablespoon soy sauce
1 tablespoon oyster sauce
1 teaspoon sugar
1 tablespoon cornflour/
   corn starch dissolved
   in 2 tablespoons cold
   water

Makes 10 buns

Pour the water into a little saucepan and add the sugar. Bring to the boil to dissolve the sugar. Allow to cool completely.

To make the filling, heat the fat in a frying pan or wok and add all the ingredients. Stir fry over a high heat for 4–5 minutes. Allow to cool completely.

Making a predough

Put the flour into a big bowl and make a well in it. Sprinkle the yeast into the well and pour on the cooled water mixture. Flick flour on the top of the water to close the well. Cover and allow to rest for 1 hour.

Making the dough

Put the remaining ingredients in the bowl with the predough. Mix together into a ball and then turn out onto the counter. Knead well for 10 minutes. Pop the dough back into the bowl and cover. Allow to rest for 2 hours.

Cut out 10 little squares of nonstick baking parchment about 5 x 5 cm/2 x 2 inches. Alternatively, you can use paper muffin cups.

Turn the dough out onto a lightly floured surface.

Shaping

Sprinkle the baking powder on top of the dough. Knead the dough well for a minute or so. Roll the dough out into a rectangle 5 mm/¼ inch thick. Fold one of the short edges into the middle and then fold the other one up over the first one to the edge, as if you were folding up a sheet of paper for an envelope. Turn the dough 45° (¼ of a turn). Roll the dough into a rectangle again and brush the whole thing with water. Starting at a long side, roll the dough up as tightly as you can into a tight sausage. Cut the sausage into 10 equal portions and allow to rest for 15 minutes under a dry tea towel.

Flatten one piece of dough into a disc about 5 cm/2 inches in diameter and brush it with sesame oil. Place 1 teaspoon of the filling in the middle of the disc. Pleat the edge of the disc and bring it up and around the filling to make a little parcel. Pinch the pleated edge tightly to seal the filling in. Place the bun, pleated-side-up, on a little square of paper and place it on a tray. Repeat this with the remaining portions of dough and filling. Cover with a dry tea towel and allow to rest for 30 minutes.

Heat water in a steamer. Place as many buns as can comfortably fit on the steamer tray, leaving space for them to spread out. Cover and steam for 30 minutes. Remove the lid quickly so drops of water don't fall on the buns. Eat warm dipped in soy sauce.

Sweet Steamed Buns China

Many people think rice is the dominant grain in China but in the North of China where it is cold and dry, the main grain grown and consumed is wheat. Much of the wheat is eaten in the form of steamed buns like these that are either served plain or stuffed.

500 g/4 cups plain/
    all-purpose white
    wheat flour
2.5 g/1¼ teaspoons
    instant yeast, 5 g/1¾
    teaspoons dry yeast, or
    10 g/0.35 oz fresh yeast
250 g/1 cup water
10 g/2½ teaspoons salt
25 g/2½ tablespoons
    sugar
1 teaspoon melted lard or
    neutral vegetable oil

Filling
jam, sweet bean paste,
    sweet sesame paste,
    kaya/coconut jam,
    coconut…whatever you
    like

Makes 16 buns

If you are using instant or fresh yeast, put all the dough ingredients into a big bowl and mix them together to form a ball. Turn the dough out onto the counter and knead it well for 10 minutes. The dough will be a bit stiff.

If you are using dry yeast, put the flour into a big bowl and make a well. Sprinkle the yeast and the sugar into the well and pour on the water. Allow to rest for 15 minutes. A beige sludge may or may not form on the top of the water. Don't worry too much, the important thing is to dissolve the yeast. Add the rest of the dough ingredients and bring them all together in a ball in the bowl. Turn the dough out onto the counter and knead it well for 10 minutes. The dough will be a bit stiff.

Pop the kneaded dough back into the bowl and cover. Allow it to rest for 2 hours.

Meanwhile cut out 16 little squares of baking parchment about 5 x 5 cm/2 x 2 inches. Alternatively, you can use paper muffin cups.

Turn the dough out onto a lightly floured surface.

Shaping

Roll the dough into a long rectangle 5 mm/¼ inch thick. Fold one of the short edges into the middle and then fold the other one up over the first one to the edge, as if you were folding up a sheet of paper for an envelope. Turn the dough 45° (¼ of a turn). Roll the dough into a rectangle again then brush the whole thing with water. Starting at a long side, roll the dough up as tightly as you can into a tight sausage. Cut the sausage into 12 equal portions and allow the portions of dough to rest for 15 minutes under a tea towel.

Flatten one piece of dough into a disc about 5 cm/2 inches in diameter and brush it with water. Place 1 teaspoon of the filling of your choice in the middle of the disc. Too much filling and the bun may burst in the steamer. Gently stretch the dough around the filling and gather the edges together to form a little parcel. Press the edges together firmly to seal the parcel. Place the parcel seam-side-down on a little square of paper and place it on a tray. Repeat for the remaining portions of dough and filling. Cover with a dry tea towel and allow to rest for 30 minutes.

Heat water in a steamer. Place as many buns as can comfortably fit on the steamer tray, leaving space for them to spread out. Cover and steam for 30 minutes. They are delicious when eaten warm.

Milk Buns Japan

Neither milk nor wheat feature heavily in the traditional Japanese diet. However, today there is plenty of bread available to buy and Japanese bakers are among the best in the world. Hokkaido is one of the Northern islands in Japan and this is where most of the milk comes from. It is no surprise then that these buns originate from there.

Scalded dough
50 g/½ cup plain/
    all-purpose white
    wheat flour
125 g/½ cup boiling water

Dough
350 g/2¾ cups plain/
    all-purpose white
    wheat flour
2 g/1 teaspoon instant
    yeast, 4 g/1¼
    teaspoons dry yeast, or
    8 g/0.28 oz fresh yeast
50 g/¼ cup white sugar
60 g/¼ cup milk, heated
    up to just below boiling
    point, then cooled to
    room temperature
8 g/2 teaspoons salt
1 egg
50 g/3 tablespoons butter

Decoration
milk, to glaze

*1 large or 2 small loaf pans,
    buttered*

Makes 8 buns

Making the scalded dough

Put the flour into a small bowl and pour over the boiling water. Stir to incorporate the flour and make a paste. Cover and allow to cool completely.

Making the dough

Put the flour into a big mixing bowl and make a well. Sprinkle the yeast and sugar into the well and pour over the cooled milk. Flick some flour over the milk to close the well and then cover. Allow to rest for 1 hour.

Add the salt, egg and cooled scalded dough (torn up into bits as this makes it easier to incorporate) to the dough and bring the ingredients together in the bowl. Turn the dough out onto the counter and knead it well for 10 minutes. Add the butter and knead for another 10 minutes. Put the dough back in the bowl, cover and allow to rest for 2 hours. This dough is pretty stiff, just so you know.

Pull the dough out onto an unfloured surface.

Shaping

Divide the dough into 8 equal portions (weigh the dough if you want buns the same size). Allow to rest for 15 minutes.

Flour the counter and a rolling pin. Roll a portion of dough into an oval about 25 cm x 7.5 cm/10 x 3 inches wide. Pick up one of the short edges and fold it into the middle and then pick up the other short edge and fold it right over the first – as if you were folding paper for an envelope.

Turn the folded dough 45° (¼ of a turn) and then flip it over. Roll it out into an oval, fold it and turn it again just as before. Roll it out into an oval for the final time, making sure the oval is no wider than your loaf pan. Roll up the oval into a tight sausage and place it seam-side-down in the buttered loaf pan.

Repeat for the remaining dough. If using a large pan, place all 8 pieces in the pan. If using 2 small pans, place 4 pieces in each pan. Cover and allow to rest for 1 hour.

Preheat the oven to 200°C (400°F) Gas 6.

Brush the tops of the buns with milk. Bake in the preheated oven for 45 minutes. Remove from the pan and allow to cool on a wire rack.

Scalded dough

100 g/¾ cup plain/
    all-purpose white
    wheat flour
70 g/⅓ cup boiling water

Dough

400 g/3¼ cups plain/
    all-purpose white
    wheat flour
2.5 g/1¼ teaspoons
    instant yeast, 5 g/1¾
    teaspoons dry yeast, or
    10 g/0.35 oz fresh yeast
80 g/6 tablespoons sugar
175 g/⅔ cup milk, heated
    up to just below boiling
    point, then cooled to
    room temperature
10 g/2½ teaspoons salt
1 egg
60 g/5 tablespoons butter,
    cubed, at room
    temperature

Filling

100 g/6½ tablespoons
    butter, divided into 12
    little cubes, at room
    temperature

Topping

125 g/8 tablespoons
    butter, at room
    temperature
125 g/1 scant cup
    icing/confectioners'
    sugar
1 egg
240 g/2 cups plain/
    all-purpose white
    wheat flour
½ teaspoon pandan paste
    or 3 tablespoons strong
    coffee (optional)

prepared baking sheets
    (see page 9)

Makes 12 buns

Mexican Coffee Buns — Malaysia

I don't think anyone knows where the name for these buns comes from. They resemble a Mexican bun called a concha and, yes, you can eat them while you drink coffee. Sound convincing? I thought not. They are sold all over Malaysia and a bakery chain called Rotiboy has made them so famous that they are often called Rotiboy buns.

Making the scalded dough

Put the flour into a little bowl and pour over the boiling water. Stir with a spoon to mix the flour and water. Cover with clingfilm/plastic wrap and set aside.

Making the dough

Put the flour into a big mixing bowl and make a well. Sprinkle the yeast and sugar into the well and then pour over the cooled milk. Flick some flour over the milk to close the well, cover and allow to rest for 1 hour.

Add the salt, egg and cooled scalded dough (break it up into bits as this makes it easier to incorporate it) to the dough and bring the ingredients together in the bowl. Turn the dough out onto the counter and knead well for 10 minutes. Add the butter and knead again for 10 minutes. Put the dough back in the bowl, cover and allow to rest for 2 hours.

Pull the dough out onto an unfloured surface.

Shaping

Divide the dough into 12 equal portions. Roll each portion into a tight ball (see page 12). Allow to rest under a dry tea towel for 15 minutes.

Gently flatten each piece of dough with your hands into a disc about 3 cm/ 1¼ inches in diameter and then place a little cube of butter in the centre. Stretch the dough around the butter, roll it up and shape into a tight ball (see page 12). Place on the prepared baking sheet. Repeat for the remaining dough.

Cover with a dry tea towel and allow to rest for 30 minutes.

Beat together the ingredients for the topping. Pipe a thin swirl on the top of each bun that starts at the top of each bun in the centre and travels one third of the way down the sides. Allow the buns to rest, uncovered, for about 15 minutes.

Preheat the oven to 220°C (425°F) Gas 7.

Pop the buns in the preheated oven and bake them for 15 minutes.

Remove from the oven and cool completely on a wire rack before eating.

Masala Buns India

Masala is a word used to describe a mixture of spices in South Asian cooking. Masala buns are savoury, enriched buns that are stuffed with something made with masala. They are eaten either as a light meal or a little snack and are perfect for picnics and lunchboxes.

300 g/2⅓ cups strong white or wholemeal/whole-wheat (bread) flour

1.5 g/¾ teaspoon instant yeast, 3 g/1 teaspoon dry yeast, or 6 g/0.2 oz fresh yeast

200 g/¾ cup plus 1 tablespoon milk, heated up to just below boiling point, then cooled to room temperature

6 g/1½ teaspoons salt

1 tablespoon ghee (clarified butter) or butter

Filling

Here is a recipe for masala potatoes that I have adapted from Vivek Singh's excellent book, *Curry: Classic and Contemporary*:

250 g/8 oz floury potatoes

30 g/2 tablespoons ghee (clarified butter) or high smoke-point vegetable oil

¼ teaspoon cumin seeds

½ small onion, diced

pinch of turmeric

5 mm/¼ inch piece of fresh ginger, peeled and finely grated

1 small green or red chilli/chile, deseeded, deveined and finely chopped

½ teaspoon salt

Decoration

milk, to glaze

sesame seeds

large frying pan

prepared baking sheets (see page 9)

Makes 8 buns

Put the flour into a big mixing bowl and make a well. Sprinkle the yeast into the well and pour over the cooled milk. Flick some flour over the milk to close the well, cover and allow to rest for 1 hour.

Add the salt and bring all of the ingredients together in the bowl. Turn the dough out onto the counter and knead it well for 10 minutes. Add the ghee or butter and knead for another 10 minutes. Put the dough back in the bowl, cover and allow to rest for 2 hours.

To make the filling, peel the potatoes and boil them until soft. Drain and allow to cool before you cut them into little cubes. Heat the fat in a large frying pan and add the cumin seeds followed by the onion. Cook over a medium heat until the onion is translucent. Add the turmeric, ginger and chilli/chile and stir for 30 seconds. Add the potatoes and salt and lower the heat. Stir gently to evenly colour the potatoes.

Remove from the heat and allow to cool completely.

Pull the dough out gently onto an unfloured surface.

Shaping

Shape the dough into a tight sausage (see page 11). Divide the sausage into 8 equal portions and allow to rest under a dry tea towel for 15 minutes.

Flatten one piece of dough with your hand into a disc about 5 mm/¼ inch thick. Brush the edge with water. Place a spoonful of filling into the centre of the disc, bring the edges of the dough together to form a parcel and pinch them firmly to seal them.

Turn it over so the seal is underneath and place it on the prepared baking sheet. Repeat with the remaining dough portions and filling. Allow to rest for 1 hour under a dry tea towel.

Preheat the oven to 220°C (425°F) Gas 7.

Brush the tops of the buns with milk and sprinkle with sesame seeds. Bake the buns in the preheated oven for 15–20 minutes.

Remove from the oven and allow to cool completely on a wire rack before you bite into them because the filling will be hot! Pack them as an alternative to sandwiches and you will be the coolest person at the picnic.

Khara Buns India

Khara means spicy in Hindi. There is no particular recipe (or rather, there are an infinite number of recipes) for khara buns. It depends on how savoury and how spicy you like them. These are not too hot so if you would like them a little spicier, add another chilli/chile! Excellent on their own or with a cup of tea in the afternoon, they are a splendid snack.

300 g/2⅓ cups strong white or wholemeal/whole-wheat (bread) flour

200 g/¾ cup plus 1 tablespoon water

1.5 g/¾ teaspoon instant yeast, 3 g/1 teaspoon dry yeast, or 6 g/0.2 oz fresh yeast

6 g/1½ teaspoons salt

30 g/2 tablespoons ghee (clarified butter) or butter

1 garlic clove, crushed

1 teaspoon cumin seeds

½ teaspoon ground coriander

1 small green or red chilli/chile, deseeded and deveined, finely chopped, or ½ teaspoon dried red pepper/chili flakes

a big handful of fresh coriander/cilantro leaves left whole

prepared baking sheets (see page 9)

Makes 8 buns

If you are using instant or fresh yeast, put all the ingredients, except the fresh coriander/cilantro, into a big mixing bowl. Bring them together into a ball in the bowl and then pull the dough out onto the counter. Knead well for 10 minutes.

If you are using dry yeast, put the flour into a bowl and make a well. Add the yeast and pour half of the water on top. Allow to rest for 15 minutes. A beige sludge may or may not form on the top of the water, but don't worry – what is important is to dissolve the yeast. Add the other ingredients, except the coriander/cilantro leaves, bring them together into a ball in the bowl and then pull the dough out onto the counter.

Return the dough to the bowl. Cover and allow to rest for 15 minutes and then fold in the coriander/cilantro leaves. Cover the dough again and allow to rest for 1½ hours.

Pull the dough out onto an unfloured surface.

Shaping

Shape the dough into a tight sausage (see page 11). Divide the sausage into 8 equal portions and allow to rest under a tea towel for 15 minutes.

Shape each portion into a tight ball (see page 12). Place each ball on the prepared baking sheet. Cover with a dry tea towel and allow to rest for 45 minutes.

Preheat the oven to 220°C (425°F) Gas 7.

Pop the buns in the preheated oven and bake for 20 minutes. Remove from the oven and allow them to cool completely on a wire rack.

Pan de Camote Peru

Camote means sweet potato in Spanish and camotes – both pale orange and white – are popular all over Latin America. They are a proud filler in these buns – making the expensive wheat flour go further – just as oats are to Maritimers' bread and cornmeal is to Anadama bread (both recipes in my first book). Additionally, camote adds flavour and makes a light, beautifully textured bun.

250 g/8 oz peeled sweet potatoes

100 g/6½ tablespoons lard or butter

650 g/5 cups plain/all-purpose white wheat flour

3 g/1½ teaspoons instant yeast, 6 g/2 teaspoons dry yeast, or 12 g/0.42 oz fresh yeast

100 g/scant ½ cup milk, heated up to just below boiling point, then cooled to room temperature

2 eggs

12 g/1 tablespoon salt

prepared baking sheets (see page 9)

Makes 16 buns

Peel and cook the sweet potatoes however you would like to (microwave, baked or boiled) and mash them with half of the lard or butter and some salt to taste. Allow to cool completely while you make the dough.

Put the flour into a bowl and make a well. Sprinkle the yeast into the well and then pour over the cooled milk. Close the well by flicking some of the flour on top of the milk and then allow to rest for 1 hour.

At the end of an hour, when the sweet potatoes are cool, add the eggs to the sweet potato and mix thoroughly. Add this to the bowl with the flour and add the salt. Bring everything together into a ball in the bowl and then turn out onto the counter. Knead well for 10 minutes and then add the remaining butter. Continue to knead for a further 10 minutes. This is a very soft dough – just persevere and don't add any more flour however much you are tempted. Return the dough to the bowl, cover and allow to rest for 2 hours.

Gently pull the dough out of the bowl onto a lightly floured surface.

Shaping

Divide the dough into 16 equal portions. Flour your hands and shape each portion into a tight ball, handling the dough gently (see page 13). Transfer the buns to the prepared baking sheet. Lightly flour the tops of the buns, cover them with a dry tea towel and allow them to rest for 45 minutes.

Preheat the oven to 220°C (425°F) Gas 7.

Pop the buns in the preheated oven and bake for 20 minutes. Remove from the oven and allow them to cool on a wire rack.

Pan Chancay Peru

These gorgeous buns come from the little town of Chancay near Lima in Peru. Legend has it that they were introduced to the country by a Spaniard but what makes them uniquely Latin American is the inclusion of raw cane sugar which colours them a light brown and gives them a distinctive caramel flavour. If you cannot get raw cane sugar, use plain white sugar and add a teaspoon of molasses. In Peru they are frequently eaten for dinner with a cup of hot chocolate or milk.

250 g/1 cup water
50 g/¼ cup raw cane
    sugar (or 50 g/¼ cup
    white sugar and
    1 teaspoon molasses)
500 g/4 cups plain/
    all-purpose white
    wheat flour
2.5 g/1¼ teaspoons
    instant yeast, 5 g/1¾
    teaspoons dry yeast, or
    10 g/0.35 oz fresh yeast
10 g/2½ teaspoons salt
1 egg
50 g/3 tablespoons lard
1 teaspoon ground
    cinnamon
1 teaspoon ground anise

Glaze
50 g/3 tablespoons melted
    butter that you have
    allowed to cool slightly

Decoration
sesame seeds

*prepared baking sheets
    (see page 9)*

Makes 12 buns

Heat the water in a small saucepan and add the sugar. Bring it to the boil and stir to dissolve the sugar thoroughly. Once there are no sugar crystals, turn the heat off and let the water cool completely.

Put the flour into a big bowl and make a well. Sprinkle in the yeast and add the cooled water and sugar mixture. Flick some flour over the top of the water to close the well and then cover the bowl. Allow to rest for 1 hour.

Sprinkle the salt around the edge of the flour and add the egg, lard and ground spices. Bring the ingredients together in the bowl into a ball. Turn the ball out onto the counter and knead well for 10 minutes. The dough will be soft and sticky.

Pop it back in the bowl, cover and allow to rest for 2 hours.

Pull the dough out onto an unfloured surface.

Shaping
Shape the dough into a tight sausage (see page 11).

Cut the dough into 12 equal pieces and allow to rest under a dry tea towel for 15 minutes. Shape each piece into a tight ball and place on the prepared baking sheet. Cover with a dry tea towel and allow to rest for 45 minutes.

Preheat the oven to 220°C (425°F) Gas 7.

Brush the buns with melted butter to glaze and then sprinkle sesame seeds on top. Pop them in the preheated oven for 15 minutes.

Remove from the oven and allow to cool completely on a wire rack before eating.

Vigilantes Uruguay

Get this: vigilantes are the snack of choice of the Uruguayan police force! That has got to be reason enough to bake them.

300 g/2⅓ cups plain/
  all-purpose white
  wheat flour
1.5 g/¾ teaspoon instant
  yeast, 3 g/1 teaspoon
  dry yeast, or 6 g/0.2 oz
  fresh yeast
200 g/¾ cup plus
  1 tablespoon milk,
  heated up to just below
  boiling point, then
  cooled to room
  temperature
6 g/1½ teaspoons salt
50 g/3 tablespoons butter

Filling
The jam of your choice.
  Preferably red. It's more
  evocative that way.

Glaze
1 egg, beaten
1 tablespoon water
pinch of salt
pinch of sugar

*prepared baking sheets
  (see page 9)*

Makes 20 buns

Put the flour into a bowl and make a well. Sprinkle the sugar and the yeast into the well and pour in the milk. Flick some flour on the surface of the milk to close the well and then cover the bowl. Allow to rest for 1 hour.

Add the salt and mix the ingredients together into a ball in the bowl. Turn this out onto the counter and knead for 10 minutes. Add the butter and knead for a further 10 minutes.

Pop the dough back into the bowl and cover it. Allow to rest for 2 hours.

Pull the dough out onto an unfloured surface.

Shaping

Divide the dough into 20 equal portions. [1] Lightly flour the counter. Gently stretch each piece of dough into a little diamond shape and place it on the counter. [2] Smear a little of the jam from the top corner to the bottom corner of the dough. [3]

Brush the edges of the dough with water and then fold the right corner over the jam and fold the left corner over the right corner to the edge of the dough. [4] Pick this up with a scraper and pop it on a prepared baking sheet, folded-side-up.

Repeat for all the other pieces of dough making sure you leave some room between each bun. Cover with a dry tea towel and allow to rest for 45 minutes.

Preheat the oven to 220°C (425°F) Gas 7.

Beat together the ingredients for the glaze. Brush the glaze over the buns and pop them in the preheated oven. Bake for 15 minutes. Remove from the oven and allow to cool completely on a wire rack before eating them. It's just a bit easy to eat too many. Now we know where the police get their robust figures from!

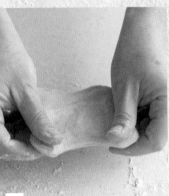

2

3

4

Bolillos Mexico

One of the staples of Mexican food is called a torta, which is a sandwich served on a bun called a bolillo. There are many kinds of tortas – one of which is even sunk in a kind of a soup! Whatever kind you like, the bolillo is the main event. It has to be crispy on the outside and fluffy on the inside and there is a strict shape. The dough is shaped for its final rise into a sausage that is 14 x 5 cm/5½ x 2 inches and has tapered ends. The final bun has a single slash down the centre. Anything else is just not a bolillo.

Predough
75 g/⅔ cup plain/
   all-purpose white
   wheat flour
40 g/2½ tablespoons
   water
pinch of yeast (any kind
   will do)

Dough
450 g/3⅔ cups plain/
   all-purpose white
   wheat flour
2.5 g/1¼ teaspoons
   instant yeast, 5 g/1¾
   teaspoons dry yeast, or
   10 g/0.35 oz fresh yeast
225 g/scant 1 cup water
50 g/3 tablespoons lard
10 g/2½ teaspoons salt

Glaze
1 teaspoon cornflour/corn
   starch dissolved in
   3 tablespoons water

*prepared baking sheets
   (see page 9)*

Makes 10 buns

Day One: making a predough

Mix the ingredients together in a bowl and cover it. Allow to rest for 12–48 hours on the counter. The longer you leave it, the stronger the flavour will be.

Day Two: making the dough

Put the flour into the bowl and make a well in it. Sprinkle the yeast into the well and add the water. Flick some flour over the water to close the well. Allow to rest for 1 hour.

Add the salt, the predough and the lard and mix it together into a ball. Pull the dough ball out of the bowl and onto the counter and knead well for 10 minutes. Pop it back into the bowl and allow to rest for 1½ hours.

Pull the dough out of the bowl and give it a good knead again to get all the air out. Pop it back in the bowl, cover and allow to rest again for 1½ hours.

Pull the dough gently out of the bowl onto an unfloured surface.

(Continued overleaf.)

In Mexico, bolillos are baked several times a day and it is the task of the children to go and buy them. The trick is to get there when the bolillos are just coming out of the oven. At some point in many an evening, I have known friends swap their childhood bolillo stories (drunken bakers, sleeping bakers, bakers who had been in a fight) and all of them remember the taste of the warm bread that they nibbled on their way home.

1

2

3

Shaping

Shape the dough into a tight sausage (see page 12).

Cut the dough into 10 equal portions, place these under a dry tea towel and allow to rest for 15 minutes.

Take a piece of dough and stretch it gently with a rolling pin into a rough oval about 13 cm/5 inches across. [1] Pick up the long, bottom edge of the oval and fold it into the middle – don't press down. [2] Take the top edge of the oval and fold it into the middle to meet the bottom edge – don't press down. [3]

Gently take the new long outside edges of the dough and bring them up towards each other to meet in the middle, pinching them together – just at the edges. The point is to not deflate the dough. [4]

With the dough seam-side-up, place the edge of both of your hands about 5 mm/¼ inch in from both ends of the bun. [5] Roll the bun back and forth on the spot and press firmly to make little 'ears' at either end of the bun. [6]

Place the bun seam-side-up on the prepared baking sheet. Repeat this for all the remaining pieces of dough. Cover with a dry tea towel and allow to rest for 1 hour. [7, 8]

Preheat the oven to 220°C (425°F) Gas 7.

Before baking, make a deep cut down the whole length of each bun and brush them with the glaze. Bake in the preheated oven for 15–20 minutes.

Remove from the oven and transfer to a wire rack to cool.

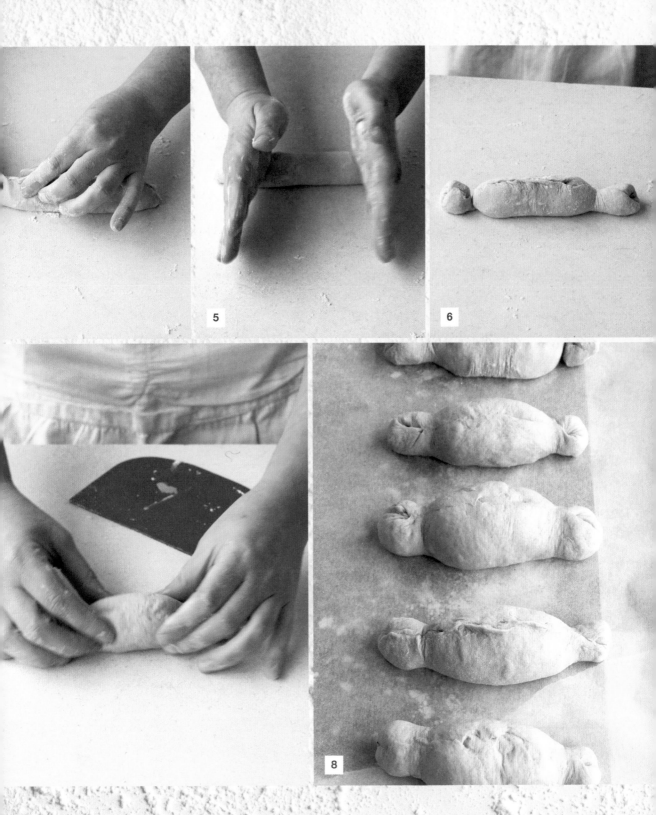

5

6

8

Starter dough

100 g/¾ cup flour (plain/
all-purpose white or
wholemeal/whole-wheat
wheat flour)

100 g/scant ½ cup water

pinch of yeast (any kind
will do)

a small cone of piloncillo
dissolved in 100 g/6½
tablespoons water OR
50 g/¼ cup white or
brown sugar plus
1 teaspoon molasses,
dissolved in 100 g/
6½ tablespoons water

Dough

350 g/2¾ cups flour (plain/
all-purpose white or
wholemeal/whole-wheat
wheat flour)

2 g/1 teaspoon instant
yeast, 4 g/1¼
teaspoons dry yeast, or
8 g/0.28 oz fresh yeast

8 g/2 teaspoons salt

1 egg

20 g/4 teaspoons lard

pinch of ground cinnamon

a handful of candied fruit
or peel, chopped

a handful of chopped nuts,
roasted in a dry frying
pan and allowed to cool
right down before you
add them

Glaze

1 egg, beaten
1 tablespoon water
pinch of sugar
pinch of salt

*prepared baking sheets
(see page 9)*

Makes 12 buns

Tlalchigual Mexico

I have only ever found these buns made in one place and that was near Lake Chapala in Mexico. Enrique and I bought them once when we were driving back to Mexico City from Puerto Vallarta. It was hardly romantic: we were at the petrol station! However, a man was selling this amazing bread from the back of his car in the car park and the aroma drew us like moths to the flame.

Day One: making the starter dough and sugar solution

Mix the flour, water and yeast together. Cover and leave it on the counter overnight.

Dissolve the piloncillo (or sugar and molasses) by simmering it gently in the water until there are no crystals left in the liquid. Remove from the heat. Cover and leave it on the counter. That way you can use it straight away when you make the dough the next day.

Day Two: making the dough

Put the flour into a big mixing bowl and make a well. Sprinkle the yeast into the well and then pour over the sugar solution. Flick some flour over the liquid to close the well and then cover and allow to rest for 1 hour.

Add the starter dough, the salt, egg, lard and cinnamon and bring the ingredients together in the bowl. Turn the dough out onto the counter and knead it well for 10 minutes. Pop it back in the bowl and cover it. Allow to rest for 30 minutes. After 30 minutes, gently fold in the fruit and nuts. Don't worry about the dough, it will recover. Once you have folded in the fruit and nuts, cover the bowl again and allow to rest for 2 hours.

Pull the dough out of the bowl gently onto an unfloured surface.

Shaping

Shape the dough into a tight sausage (see page 11). Cut the sausage into 12 equal portions. Allow to rest under a dry tea towel for 15 minutes.

Roll each portion of dough into a tight ball (see page 12) and place each ball onto the prepared baking sheet. Cover with a tea towel and allow to rest for 45 minutes.

Preheat the oven to 220°C (425°F) Gas 7.

Beat together the ingredients for the glaze and brush each bun generously with it. Pop them in the preheated oven and bake for 15 minutes. Remove from the oven and allow to cool completely on a wire rack.

Easiest Buns in the World USA

I confess I am not a fan of the end-result of the 'no knead' method of making bread. I am a kneader: I like the texture of kneaded bread better. However, the 'no knead' method is very popular and, even for committed kneaders, it has a time and a place: when you know you will be in a rush.

650 g/5 cups plain/
  all-purpose white or
  wholemeal/wholewheat
  wheat or spelt flour
  (or a mixture)
600 g/2½ cups water
2 g/1 teaspoon instant
  yeast, 4 g/1¼
  teaspoons dry yeast, or
  8 g/0.28 oz fresh yeast
12 g/1 tablespoon salt
a handful of seeds, nuts,
  or dried fruit, chopped
  (optional)

*prepared baking sheets
  (see page 9)*

Makes 16 buns

The night before you want your buns, measure all the ingredients into a big bowl and give it a good stir to make sure everything is well mixed.

Cover the bowl with clingfilm/plastic wrap and pop it in the fridge. Go to bed.

Shaping

In the morning, preheat the oven to 220°C (425°F) Gas 7. Go and brush your teeth while the oven heats up and contemplate how many buns you need that day (for breakfast, lunch, a picnic…).

Return to the kitchen and take the bowl out of the fridge. Exclaim in delight when you see how the dough is all puffy. [1]

Using 2 spoons, drop blobs of dough onto the baking sheet, 'stacking' them as best you can so the buns are more round than flat. [2, 3] You do not need to use all the dough. It will last in the fridge for 2–3 days which means you can have fresh buns every morning over that time (and then you can make more dough).

Pop them in the preheated oven and bake for 20 minutes. Have a shower. Take them out of the oven.

Allow to cool completely on a wire rack while you get dressed.

1   2   3

Montreal Bagels Canada

There is a huge difference between Montreal bagels and New York bagels that people outside of Eastern Canada may not know. Montreal bagels are flatter, denser and sweeter than their New York cousins. They are boiled in a light syrup and are always baked in a wood oven. Don't let that put you off – these bagels are amazing when baked in a conventional oven too.

750 g/5⅓ cups strong
  white (bread) flour
350 g/1½ cups water
3 g/1½ teaspoons instant
  yeast, 6 g/2 teaspoons
  dry yeast, or 12 g/
  0.42 oz fresh yeast
15 g/4 teaspoons salt
2 egg yolks (save the
  whites for the glaze)
100 g/6½ tablespoons
  malt syrup (you can
  substitute honey)

For the steaming
2 litres/2 quarts water
100 g/6½ tablespoons
  malt syrup (you can
  substitute honey)

Glaze
2 egg whites
2 tablespoons water

Decoration
sesame seeds

large saucepan
prepared baking sheets
  (see page 9)

Makes 12 buns

If you are using instant or fresh yeast, put all the ingredients into a big bowl and mix them together into a ball in the bowl. Pull the dough out onto the counter and knead it for 10 minutes. It is quite a stiff dough so just persevere.

If you are using dry yeast, put the flour into a bowl and make a well. Sprinkle in the yeast, add 100 g/scant ½ cup of the water and allow to rest for 10–15 minutes. A beige sludge may or may not form on the top of the water – it does not matter as long as the yeast is dissolved. Add all the other ingredients and mix them together into a ball in the bowl. Pull the dough out onto the counter and knead it for 10 minutes. It is quite a stiff dough so just persevere.

Pop the dough back in the bowl, cover and allow to rest for 2 hours.

Gently pull the dough out onto an unfloured surface and shape it into a tight sausage (see page 11).

(Continued overleaf.)

Arguably the most famous of all Montreal bagel bakeries is up on the 'plateau'. This is a vibrant, multi-cultural neighbourhood in which everyone, from students on bikes to wealthy Montreallers in fancy cars, queues up at the St Viateur bagel bakery. They have been boiling and baking their bagels 24 hours a day for over 50 years.

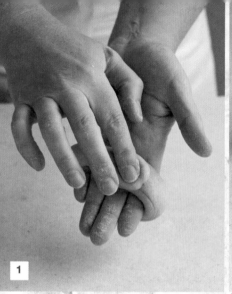
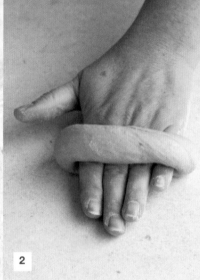

Shaping

Divide the dough into 12 equal portions and allow to rest for 5 minutes under a dry tea towel.

Take one piece of dough and roll it into a snake about 30 cm/12 inches long. Wrap the snake around your hand so that the 2 ends meet in your palm. [1]

Place your palm (with the overlapping ends of the dough in it) on the counter and roll it firmly back and forth to seal the ends. [2]

Place the formed bagel on a lightly floured surface and cover it with a dry tea towel. Repeat with all the remaining pieces of dough. Allow them to rest for 45 minutes.

Preheat the oven to 220°C (425°F) Gas 7.

Bring the water and malt syrup to simmering point in a large saucepan. Press the bagels quite firmly to flatten them out to a thickness of only about 1 cm/ ½ inch (you don't want puffy, airy bagels, but dense chewy bagels) and then place them into the simmering solution. Put as many as will comfortably fit into the saucepan and simmer them for 30 seconds. [3]

Turn them over as you remove them from the water and place them on the prepared baking sheet. To glaze, lightly beat together the egg whites and water and brush it on the buns. Sprinkle sesame seeds on top.

Pop them in the preheated oven and bake for 20–25 minutes. Remove from the oven. Try to cool them completely on a wire rack before eating them. They are delicious with butter and jam, cream cheese and smoked salmon, anything or nothing at all.

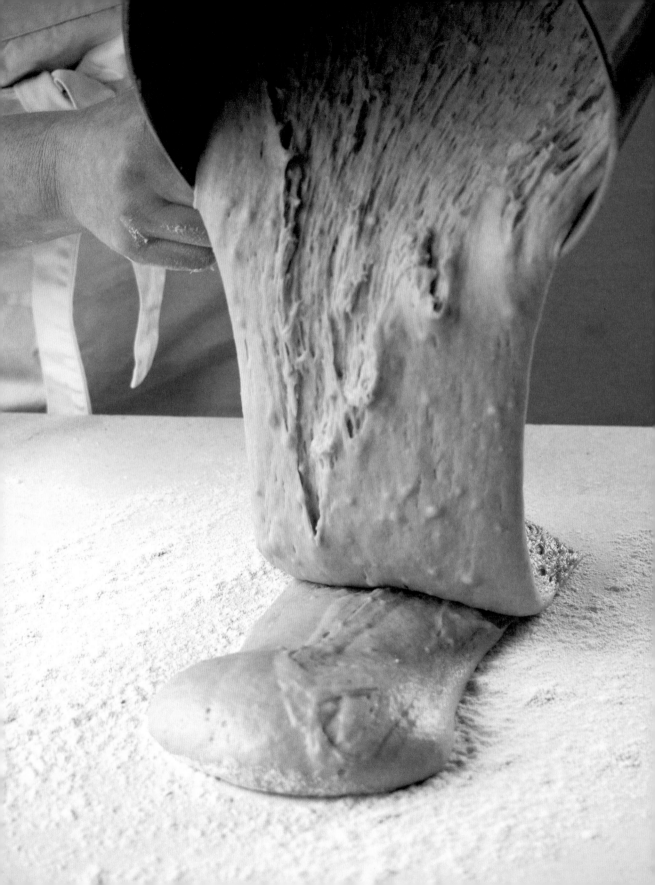

Occasional Buns

250 g/1⅔ cups raisins

Dough

150 g/1 cup plain/
  all-purpose wholemeal/
  whole-wheat flour
300 g/2⅔ cups plain/
  all-purpose white
  wheat flour
2 g/1⅛ teaspoons instant
  yeast, 4.5 g/1½
  teaspoons dry yeast, or
  9 g/0.3 oz fresh yeast
50 g/¼ cup sugar
280 g/1¼ cups milk,
  heated up to just below
  boiling point, then
  cooled to room
  temperature
1 egg
9 g/2¼ teaspoons salt
2 teaspoons ground
  cinnamon
1 teaspoon ground mixed
  spice
1 teaspoon ground ginger
½ teaspoon ground cloves
½ teaspoon ground
  allspice
50 g/3 tablespoons butter

Crosses mix

50 g/⅓ cup plain/
  all-purpose white
  wheat flour
pinch of baking powder
½ teaspoon vegetable oil
  of your choice
50 g/3½ tablespoons cold
  water

Glaze

liquid honey or golden
  syrup

*prepared baking sheets
  (see page 9)*

Makes 16 buns

Hot Cross Buns UK

This recipe for Hot Cross Buns appeared in my first book, but it is such a classic, it just had to be included here. This is traditionally an Easter bun and I hope you agree that the homemade variety is infinitely superior to the shop-bought one. You might like it so much that you make it all year round. You can leave off the crosses and just call them not cross buns, if you prefer.

Put the raisins in a little bowl and just cover them with water (or rum or brandy if you would like a grown-up hot cross bun). Give them a little stir every once in a while.

Put the flours in a big mixing bowl and make a well. Sprinkle the yeast and sugar into the well and pour over the cooled milk. Flick some of the flour over the top of the milk to close the well and allow to rest for 1 hour.

Add the egg, salt and spices and gather the dough together into a ball. Turn it out onto the counter and knead well for 10 minutes. Add the butter and continue to knead for 10 minutes. The mixture will be sticky but don't let that stop you and please don't add more flour. Pop it back in the bowl, cover and allow to rest for 15 minutes.

Drain the raisins and gently squish them into the dough trying not to smear them. Pop the dough back into the bowl, cover and allow it to rest for 2 hours, until it has doubled in size.

Pull the dough out gently onto an unfloured surface.

Shaping

Divide the dough into 16 equal portions (each about 75 g/3 oz). Shape into tight balls (see page 12). Place about 5 cm/2 inches apart on a prepared baking sheet. Flour the tops lightly, cover them with a dry tea towel and allow to rest for 45 minutes or so.

Preheat the oven to 200°C (400°F) Gas 6.

To make the crosses, whisk all the ingredients together in a little bowl. Scrape the crossing mixture into a piping bag or a little polythene food bag and cut a tiny hole in one corner. Squeeze the bag gently to get all the mixture gathered near the hole and then carefully pipe crosses on each risen bun.

Pop them in the preheated oven and bake for 18–20 minutes. In an ideal world this results in a brown bun and a white cross. Take them out of the oven and put them on a cooling rack that is sitting on top of some greaseproof paper. Brush the buns immediately with liquid honey, golden syrup or the glaze of your choice.

Iced Buns UK

This is a classic English bun that you can find in any good, traditional bake shop (along with jammy doughnuts, Eccles cakes, cream slices, sausage rolls and other good things). There is something rather sentimental about iced buns. They remind people of childhood occasions – birthday parties, special teas, and days out with granny. They are easy to make and shape, are rather plain (no polluting influence of nuts, raisins or spices) and have a thick coating of shiny, white icing on the top that you can lick off at your leisure. They are great buns to make with children.

500 g/3¾ cups plain/
all-purpose white
wheat flour
75 g/6 tablespoons sugar
2.5 g/1¼ teaspoons
instant yeast, 5 g/1¾
teaspoons dry yeast, or
10 g/0.35 oz fresh yeast
300 g/1¼ cups milk,
heated up to just below
boiling point, then
cooled to room
temperature
10 g/2½ teaspoons salt
1 egg
75 g/5 tablespoons butter

Decoration
225 g/1⅔ cups icing/
confectioners' sugar
2 tablespoons water
hundreds and thousands/
sprinkles, coloured rock
sugar or glacé/candied
cherries, cut into small
bits, to sprinkle
(optional)

*prepared baking sheets
(see page 9)*

Makes 12 buns

Put the flour into a big mixing bowl and make a well. Add the sugar and yeast to the well and pour in the milk. Close the well by flicking some flour over the surface of the milk, then cover and allow to rest for 1 hour.

Sprinkle the salt around the edge of the flour and add the egg. Mix in the bowl to form a ball and then turn the dough onto the counter. Knead for 10 minutes. Add the butter and knead for another 10 minutes. Pop the dough back into the bowl and cover. Allow to rest for 2 hours.

Pull the dough out gently onto an unfloured surface.

Shaping

Divide the dough into 12 equal portions and shape each portion into a tight ball (see page 12). Cover and allow to rest for 15 minutes.

Rock each ball back and forth to elongate them into sausages and place them on a prepared baking sheet. Cover the buns with a dry tea towel and allow to rest for 1 hour.

Preheat the oven to 220°C (425°F) Gas 7.

Bake the buns in the preheated oven for 20 minutes. Remove them from the oven and allow to cool completely on a wire rack. While they are cooling, mix together the icing/confectioners' sugar and water for the icing.

When the buns are completely cool, ice them, and then decorate them if you wish.

Lincolnshire Plum Buns UK

These delicious, filling buns are worthy of anybody's bakery or kitchen and yet, they are little known outside their native Lincolnshire. Delicious with lashings of butter and even better with a slab of good Lincolnshire cheese, these buns are a fantastic addition to the High Tea table.

For the soaked fruit
strong black tea
300 g/10 oz (about 2 cups)
    mixed dried fruit of your
    choice (note: no plums –
    go figure!)

Dough
450 g/3⅔ cups plain/
    all-purpose white
    wheat flour
2.5 g/1¼ teaspoons
    instant yeast, 5 g/1¾
    teaspoons dry yeast, or
    10 g/0.35 oz fresh yeast
50 g/¼ cup brown sugar
125 g/½ cup milk, heated
    up to just below boiling
    point, then cooled to
    room temperature
100 g/6½ tablespoons
    butter, melted
10 g/2½ teaspoons salt
2 eggs
1½ teaspoons ground
    cinnamon
1½ teaspoons ground
    allspice
½ teaspoon vanilla extract

Decoration
milk, to glaze

*prepared baking sheets
    (see page 9)*

Makes 16 buns

Day One: soak the fruit

Make a fresh pot of black tea and allow it to stew for a while. Pour it over the fruit while the tea is just warm. Cover and leave it overnight.

Day Two: making the dough

Put the flour into a big bowl and make a well. Sprinkle the yeast and sugar into the well and pour over the milk. Flick some flour on top of the milk to close the well. Cover and allow to rest for 1 hour.

While you wait, melt the butter and allow it to cool right down.

Sprinkle the salt around the edge of the flour and add the eggs, melted butter, vanilla extract and spices. Bring everything together into a ball in the bowl and then turn it out onto the counter and knead well for 10 minutes. Pop it back in the bowl, cover it and allow to rest for 30 minutes.

Drain the soaked fruit. Pull the dough out of the bowl and add in the fruit gently to minimize squashing it. This takes time as there is a lot of fruit. Be patient. It can be done. Pop it back into the bowl and cover it. Allow to rest for 2 hours.

Pull the dough gently out of the bowl onto an unfloured surface.

Shaping

Divide the dough into 16 equal portions and shape each portion into a tight ball (see page 12). Place on a prepared baking sheet and dust lightly with flour. Cover with a dry tea towel and allow to rest for 45 minutes.

Preheat the oven to 220°C (425°F) Gas 7.

Brush the buns with milk before popping them into the oven. Bake them for 20 minutes. Check them after 15 minutes to make sure they are not getting too brown or the fruit is not getting too charred. If so, cover them with baking parchment or aluminium foil.

Remove from the oven and cool completely on a wire rack before eating. These keep well – they should do, with all that fruit!

Saffron Buns UK

Saffron was introduced to England by returning crusaders in the Middle Ages and presumably we have been baking these buns ever since. Saffron is expensive but a little goes a long way.

Flavoured milk
150 g/scant ⅔ cup milk
pinch of saffron threads
40 g/3 tablespoons sugar

Dough
300 g/2⅓ cups plain/
   all-purpose white
   wheat flour
1.5 g/¾ teaspoon instant
   yeast, 3 g/1 teaspoon
   dry yeast, or 6 g/0.2 oz
   fresh yeast
50 g/¼ cup sugar
6 g/1½ teaspoons salt
1 egg
30 g/2 tablespoons lard
30 g/2 tablespoons butter
   at room temperature,
   cubed
50 g/⅓ cup dark raisins (or
   sultanas/golden raisins,
   whatever you fancy or
   have on hand) soaked in
   water overnight, or while
   your dough is resting if
   you have forgotten to
   soak them the night
   before

Decoration
milk, to glaze

*prepared baking sheets
   (see page 9)*

Makes 12 buns

Flavour the milk

Put the milk into a little saucepan and add the saffron threads and sugar. Bring it just to boiling point, stirring constantly to dissolve the sugar and make sure the milk does not boil. Turn off the heat, cover it so a skin does not form, and allow it to cool down completely.

Making a predough

Put the flour into a big mixing bowl and make a well. Sprinkle the yeast and sugar into the well and then pour over the cooled milk. Flick some flour over the well to close it and then cover it with a tea towel. Allow to rest for 1 hour.

Making the dough

Add the salt, egg and lard to the predough and bring the ingredients together in the bowl. Turn the dough out on the counter and knead well for 10 minutes. Add the butter and knead again for 10 minutes. Put it back in the bowl, cover and allow to rest for 30 minutes.

Drain the soaked raisins and dump them on top of the dough in the bowl. Work them in gently so that you don't squash them. Don't worry about the dough – it will be fine. Once the raisins are worked in, cover the bowl again and allow to rest for 2 hours.

Pull the dough out gently onto an unfloured surface.

Shaping

Divide the dough into 12 equal portions. Shape each portion into a tight ball (see page 12) and place them on a prepared baking sheet. Cover with a dry tea towel and allow to rest for 45 minutes.

Preheat the oven to 220°C (425°F) Gas 7.

Flatten each bun slightly with your hand so they are no more than 3 cm/1¼ inches high and brush them with milk, before popping them into the preheated oven for 15 minutes.

Remove from the oven and allow to cool completely on a wire rack. To serve, split open and spread liberally with clotted cream, butter, jam or all three.

Chelsea Buns UK

This is another classic bun that appeared in my first book. However, as with the recipe for Hot Cross Buns, a book of buns would not be complete without it. Enjoy these delicious English buns with a cup of strong milky tea for that complete English experience.

300 g/2¼ cups plain/
  all-purpose white
  wheat flour
1.5 g/¾ teaspoon instant
  yeast, 3 g/1 teaspoon
  dry yeast, or 6 g/0.2 oz
  fresh yeast
50 g/¼ cup sugar
200 g/¾ cup milk, heated
  up to just below boiling
  point, then cooled to
  room temperature
6 g/1½ teaspoons salt
50 g/3 tablespoons butter

Filling
75 g/½ cup dried fruit
  (raisins or sultanas/
  golden raisins or
  currants or a mixture)
25 g/2½ tablespoons dried
  mixed peel, chopped
50 g/¼ cup soft brown or
  demerara sugar
25 g/2 tablespoons melted
  butter, cooled

Glaze
2 big spoonfuls of honey,
  melted

*prepared baking sheets
  (see page 9)*

Makes 8–12 buns

Put the flour into a big bowl and make a well. Sprinkle the yeast and sugar into the well and pour over the milk. Flick some flour over the surface of the milk to close the well, cover and allow to rest for 1 hour.

Add the salt and gather the ingredients into a big ball. Turn out onto the counter and knead well for 10 minutes. Add the butter and knead for another 10 minutes. Pop the dough back in the bowl, cover it and allow to rest for 2 hours.

Meanwhile, mix the dried fruit, peel and sugar together for the filling. Melt the butter and allow it to cool.

Pull the dough out gently onto a floured surface.

Shaping

Roll the dough into a big rectangle about 30 x 23 cm/12 x 9 inches. Brush it with the cooled melted butter and sprinkle the sugar and fruit mixture evenly on top to coat it.

Roll the dough up, tugging it gently towards you at each roll to achieve a tight sausage. Cut the sausage into 8–12 slices (see page 14). Place the slices on a prepared baking sheet and lightly flour the tops. Cover with a tea towel and allow to rest for 1 hour.

Preheat the oven to 220°C (425°F) Gas 7.

Pop the buns in the preheated oven. Bake them for 15 minutes, until they are golden brown. Remove from the oven and brush with melted honey while they are still hot. Cool on a wire rack.

Grittibanz Switzerland

Grittibanz are little bread men and they are eaten all over the German-speaking part of Switzerland to celebrate the feast day of St Nicholas, which falls on 6 December. In the few days coming up to 6 December you see them in all the shops and bakeries decorated with raisins, mixed peel, or even chocolate chips! They are also eaten as a savoury bun – rather like brioche – to accompany a special meal on the big day.

250 g/2 cups plain/all-purpose white wheat flour

2.5 g/1¼ teaspoons instant yeast, 5 g/1¾ teaspoons dry yeast, or 10 g/0.35 oz fresh yeast

15 g/1 tablespoon plus 1 teaspoon sugar

50 g/3 tablespoons milk, heated up to just below boiling point, then cooled to room temperature

5 g/1¼ teaspoons salt

2 eggs

100 g/6½ tablespoons unsalted butter, cut into small cubes

Decoration
a few raisins
milk

prepared baking sheets (see page 9)

Makes 4 big or 8 small buns

Put the flour into a bowl and make a well. Sprinkle the yeast and sugar into the well and pour over the milk. Flick some flour over the milk to close the well and cover. Allow to rest for 1 hour.

Sprinkle the salt around the edge of the flour and add the eggs into the well. Mix everything together and then turn it out of the bowl. Knead well for 10 minutes. Add the butter. There is no easy way to say this, just blob it in, begin to knead and keep going. The butter will melt, the dough will stick and then become a puddle on the table, you will panic and think you have done something wrong but you have not. Keep going. Use a dough scraper to pull the puddle of dough back again over and over again and keep stretching it and pushing it out. Scrape it in, push it out. The structure will eventually change and the dough will start to shine and go from pale yellow to a yellowy-brown colour and all will be well. This may take 15–20 minutes of hard work!

When the dough really changes in structure and colour, becoming a lot like golden-coloured chewing gum, scrape it back into the bowl, cover and allow it to rest on the counter for 3–4 hours until it has doubled in size.

Pull the dough out gently onto a floured surface.

(Continued overleaf.)

1

2

3

4

Shaping

Divide the dough into 4 equal portions if you want large grittibanz or 8 equal portions if you want small ones. Shape each portion gently into a loose ball (see page 12) and allow to rest for 15 minutes under a dry tea towel.

Take a piece of dough and pop it onto a lightly floured part of the counter. Gently stretch it out or roll it out with a floury rolling into a rough rectangle or oblong. [1]

Using a knife or a scraper begin to cut out your little man. First, for his legs, make a cut in the middle of the bottom of the rectangle halfway up the length of the rectangle. On the left and the right sides make two diagonal cuts, one above the other, about one third of the way down the rectangle to form his arms. [2, 3]

Spread his limbs out a bit so they don't stick together while he rises and bakes and do a bit of shaping to form his head. [4]

Place onto a prepared baking sheet and repeat with the other portions of dough. [5]

Allow to rest under a dry tea towel for 1 hour.

Preheat the oven to 180°C (350°F) Gas 4.

Before you pop the men in the oven, gently push in raisins for their eyes (so they can see where to leave the toys, of course) and their buttons (it's cold in Zurich in December) and then glaze them with milk.

Bake in the preheated oven for 25 minutes until the grittibanz are golden brown. Remove from the oven and allow to cool completely on a wire rack.

Die Brötchen von Meiner Großmutter   Germany

I am not at all sure who's großmutter (grandmother) made these buns. Mine did not, probably because she was too busy making streusel kuchen, the recipe for which is in my first book. However, lots of grandmothers must have been making these, or at least a version of these, for them to have been given this name. A plain, yeasty bun, perfect for having with Kaffee und Kuchen when you need a change from cake.

500 g/4 cups plain/
   all-purpose white
   wheat flour
2.5 g/1¼ teaspoons
   instant yeast, 5 g/1¾
   teaspoons dry yeast, or
   10 g/0.35 oz fresh yeast
150 g/¾ cup sugar
250 g/1 cup milk, heated
   up to just below boiling
   point, then cooled to
   room temperature
10 g/2½ teaspoons salt
1 egg
grated zest of 1 large,
   unwaxed lemon (2 if you
   like lemony things)
100 g/6½ tablespoons
   butter, melted and
   allowed to cool
100 g/⅔ cup dark raisins
   (or sultanas/golden
   raisins, whatever you
   fancy or have on hand),
   soaked in water or the
   alcohol of your choice
   overnight, or while your
   dough is resting if you
   have forgotten to soak
   them the night before

Glaze
1 egg
1 tablespoon water
pinch of salt
pinch of sugar

*prepared baking sheets
   (see page 9)*

Makes 12 buns

Put the flour into a big mixing bowl and make a well. Sprinkle the yeast and sugar into the well and pour over the milk. Flick some flour over the milk to close the well, cover and allow to rest for 1 hour.

Add the salt, egg, lemon zest and melted butter and bring the ingredients together in the bowl. Turn the dough out on the counter and knead it well for 10 minutes. Put it back in the bowl, cover and allow to rest for 30 minutes.

Drain the soaked raisins and dump them on top of the dough in the bowl. Work them in gently so you don't squash them. Don't worry about the dough, it will be fine. Worry about the raisins. Once the raisins are worked in, cover the bowl again and allow the dough to rest for 2 hours.

Pull the dough gently out onto an unfloured surface.

Shaping

Divide the dough into 12 equal portions. Shape each portion into a tight ball (see page 12) and place them on a prepared baking sheet. Cover with a dry tea towel and allow to rest for 45 minutes.

Preheat the oven to 220°C (425°F) Gas 7.

Beat together the ingredients for the glaze and generously brush the tops of the buns with the glaze before popping them into the preheated oven for 15 minutes. Remove from the oven and cool completely on a wire rack.

Skillingsboller Norway

These buns are technically from Norway but can be found all over the Nordic lands. The name means 'shilling buns' but I have no idea if that would have classified them as cheap or expensive!

500 g/4 cups plain/
 all-purpose white
 wheat flour
2.5 g/1¼ teaspoons
 instant yeast, 5 g/1¾
 teaspoons dry yeast, or
 10 g/0.35 oz fresh yeast
75 g/⅓ cup sugar
250 g/1 cup milk, heated
 up to just below boiling
 point, then cooled to
 room temperature
10 g/2½ teaspoons salt
1 egg
1 teaspoon ground or
 crushed cardamom
75 g/5 tablespoons butter,
 cubed, at room
 temperature

Filling
100 g/6½ tablespoons
 butter, at room
 temperature
100 g/½ cup sugar (brown
 or white)
1 teaspoon ground
 cinnamon
200 g/1⅔ cups flaked/
 slivered almonds

Glaze
1 egg
1 tablespoon water
pinch of salt
pinch of sugar

Topping
extra sugar (rock sugar if
 you can get it, regular
 sugar if you cannot)

*prepared baking sheets
 (see page 9)*

Makes 12 buns

Making a predough

Put the flour into a big mixing bowl and make a well. Sprinkle the yeast and sugar into the well and pour over the cooled milk. Flick some flour over the milk to close the well, cover and allow to rest for 1 hour.

Making a dough

After it has rested, add the salt, egg and cardamom and bring the ingredients together in the bowl. Turn the dough out onto the counter and knead it well for 10 minutes. Add the butter and knead for another 10 minutes. Put it back in the bowl, cover and allow it to rest for 2 hours.

Meanwhile, beat the butter, sugar and cinnamon together for the filling. Cover and set aside until you need it. Next, toast the flaked/slivered almonds in a dry frying pan, stirring them all the while until they are just golden brown. Don't take your eye off them for a second or they will burn and that bitter taste will enter the bread too. When they are done, remove them from the pan and set aside to cool down.

Pull the dough gently out onto a floured surface.

Shaping

Using a floury rolling pin, roll the dough into a rectangle about 60 x 30 cm/ 24 x 12 inches. Using a scraper, gently spread the filling evenly all over the dough, right to the edges. This is harder than it sounds so just be patient. Scatter the toasted almonds over the top of the filling. From a short edge of the rectangle, roll up the dough as tightly as you can, gently stretching it towards you as you roll it up. Cut the dough into 12 equal slices (see page 14). Place each slice on the prepared baking sheet and cover them with a dry tea towel. Allow to rest for 45 minutes.

Preheat the oven to 220°C (425°F) Gas 7.

Beat together the ingredients for the glaze and brush the top of each bun with it. Sprinkle sugar over the tops generously. Bake them in the preheated oven for 15 minutes. Remove from the oven and allow to cool completely on a wire rack.

Panini al Pomodoro Italy

Italy has a vast array of gorgeous buns, both sweet and savoury and in countless shapes. In typical Italian fashion, the buns are beautiful and reflect the artistry of each region (even each village!). These are among my very favourite buns from Italy – or anywhere, in fact.

Predough
75 g/⅔ cup plain/
    all-purpose white
    wheat flour
50 g/3 tablespoons water
pinch of yeast (any kind
    will do)

Dough
50 g/3 tablespoons olive
    oil
1 small onion, diced
1½ tablespoons tomato
    paste
500 g/4 cups plain/
    all-purpose white
    wheat flour
2.5 g/1¼ teaspoons
    instant yeast, 5 g/1¾
    teaspoons dry yeast, or
    10 g/0.35 oz fresh yeast
10 g/2½ teaspoons salt
250 g/1 cup water

Decoration
olive oil
tomato paste
a handful of fresh herbs
    (rosemary, oregano,
    basil, thyme, whatever
    you have on hand),
    chopped

*prepared baking sheets
    (see page 9)*

Makes 12 buns

Day One: making the predough

Put the ingredients for the predough into a small bowl and give them a stir. Cover and allow to rest for 12–24 hours.

Day Two: making the dough

Warm a small saucepan over a medium heat. Pour in 1 tablespoon of the olive oil and allow it to heat up before adding the onion. Put the lid on the saucepan and lower the heat. Sweat the onion for 10 minutes, being careful not to let it burn. Turn off the heat and stir in the tomato paste. Allow to cool.

Pour the water over the predough and mush it around with your hands to make a milky paste. Put the flour into a big mixing bowl and make a well. Sprinkle the yeast into the well. Pour in the milky paste, cover and allow to rest for 1 hour.

Add the salt and the remaining olive oil and bring the ingredients together in the bowl. Pull them onto the counter and knead well for 10 minutes. Return the dough to the bowl, cover and allow to rest for 20 minutes. Add the tomato and onion mixture and squish it into the dough, distributing it well. Cover and allow to rest for 1–2 hours or until it has doubled in size.

Pull the dough out gently onto an unfloured surface.

Shaping

Shape the dough into a tight sausage (see page 11). Divide the dough into 12 equal portions and allow them to rest under a dry tea towel for 15 minutes. Shape into tight balls (see page 12) and allow to rest under a dry tea towel for 45 minutes.

Preheat the oven to 220°C (425°F) Gas 7.

Brush each bun with a light coating of olive oil and decorate with a little blob of tomato paste and a sprinkle of fresh herbs. Pop them in the preheated oven and bake for 20 minutes. Remove from the oven and allow to cool completely on a wire rack.

Dolce Milanese Italy

Milan is one of the few places in Italy I know reasonably well. This is a great outcome of my past career when I used to go there on business pretty regularly. I certainly got to know where and what to eat, and these delicious, rich buns are something we definitely ate! They are full of butter and raisins and they are made more interesting by the sneaky shot of rum or brandy that is in there. Of course you can leave it out – but if you do you will be missing something rather special. For some reason we always ate these while drinking white wine. Don't ask me why, but it works.

For the soaked fruit
500 g/1 lb (about 3¼ cups)
  raisins

Dough
250 g/2 cups plain/
  all-purpose white
  wheat flour
1.25 g/¾ teaspoon instant
  yeast, 2.5 g/1 teaspoon
  dry yeast, or 5 g/0.17 oz
  fresh yeast
25 g/2½ tablespoons
  sugar
150 g/⅔ cup of the raisin
  water
5 g/1¼ teaspoons salt
1 tablespoon rum or
  brandy
1 tablespoon grated
  orange zest
100 g/6½ tablespoons
  butter, cubed

Glaze
1 egg
1 tablespoon water
pinch of salt
pinch of sugar

*prepared baking sheets
  (see page 9)*

Makes 20 buns

Soak the raisins in plenty of water and leave on the counter overnight.

The next day, make the dough. Put the flour into a big mixing bowl and make a well. Sprinkle the yeast and the sugar into the well. Drain the raisins, reserving the water, and then put 150 g/⅔ cup of the raisin water into the well. Drink the rest of the liquid or throw it away. Close the well by flicking some flour on top of the water and cover the bowl. Allow to rest for 1 hour.

Add the salt, rum or brandy and orange zest and bring everything together in the bowl in a big ball. Tip it out onto the counter and knead well for 10 minutes. Add the butter, bit by bit, kneading it in as you go. It will get soft and sticky but don't panic and don't add more flour. After 15–20 minutes or so, all the butter will be incorporated, the dough will be a dark yellow and it will begin to gleam. A scraper definitely helps the kneading process.

Put the dough back into the bowl, cover and allow to rest for 6 hours.

Pull the dough out gently onto a well floured surface.

(Continued overleaf.)

Shaping

Flour a rolling pin and gently roll the dough into a rectangle that is about 5 mm/¼ inch thick. [1] Scatter a third of the soaked raisins over the dough. [2] Fold one of the long sides into the middle of the dough. A scraper will help you do this. [3] Fold the other long side in to meet the other side so they just touch. [4]

Flour the counter around the dough and roll it out to widen it again into a rectangle. [5, 6] It won't be as wide as the original rectangle and that's okay. Scatter over another third of the raisins. Fold and roll as above. Scatter over the final third of the raisins. Fold in the edges, flour the top of the dough and flip it over so it is seam-side-down. [7]

Flour the top of the dough, cover it with a dry tea towel and allow it to rest for 20 minutes.

Cut the dough into 2 long strips with a knife, scraper or pizza cutter and then cut each strip into 10 pieces. Place on the prepared baking sheet. Cover and allow to rest for 20 minutes.

Preheat the oven to 220°C (425°F) Gas 7.

Beat together the ingredients for the glaze and brush the buns before popping them in the preheated oven. Bake them for 20 minutes, checking them when there are a few minutes to go and covering them with some aluminium foil or baking parchment if they are getting too brown. Remove from the oven and allow to cool completely on a wire rack before eating them.

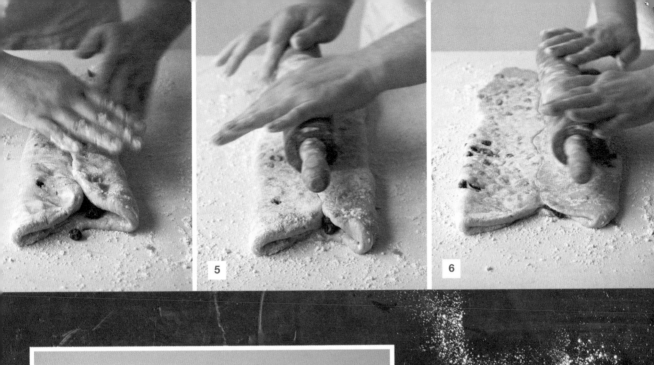

Bollos de Chicharrones Spain

Chicharron is one of life's great foods. It is pig skin deep-fried in pig fat. Pork scratchings is another name for it and if you think that's gross you either don't eat the crackling on the outside of the pork roast (nearly the same thing), are vegetarian, or have not tried it. Eat these buns while you drink dry sherry and pretend to be soaking up the sun in Extramadura, western Spain.

Predough
100 g/¾ cup plain/all-purpose white wheat flour
100 g/scant ½ cup water
pinch of yeast (any kind will do)

Dough
400 g/3¼ cups plain/all-purpose white wheat flour
4 tablespoons polenta or semolina
2 g/1 teaspoon instant yeast, 4 g/1¼ teaspoons dry yeast, or 8 g/0.28 oz fresh yeast
300 g/1¼ cups milk, heated up to just below boiling point, then cooled to room temperature
8 g/2 teaspoons salt
1 teaspoon ground cinnamon
1 teaspoon ground anise
50 g/3 tablespoons lard
100 g/3½ oz chicharron, crumbled into small bits

prepared baking sheets (see page 9)

Makes 16 buns

Day One: making a predough

Mix the ingredients together in a big bowl, cover with clingfilm/plastic wrap and leave on the counter overnight.

Day Two: making the dough

Mix the flour and polenta or semolina together and then pour this mixture into a big bowl. Make a well and sprinkle the yeast into the well. Pour over the milk and then close the well by flicking some of the flour on top of the milk. Cover and allow to rest for 1 hour.

Add all the remaining ingredients, including the predough and chicharron, and gather them together into a big ball. Turn this out onto the counter and knead well for 10 minutes. You will crush the chicharron into the dough and that is okay. The dough is quite dry so you have to work hard. Cover the bowl again and allow to rest for 2 hours.

Pull the dough gently out onto an unfloured surface.

Shaping

Divide the dough into 2 equal portions and form each portion into a tight sausage (see page 11). Cover with a dry tea towel and allow to rest for 15 minutes.

Divide each sausage into 8 pieces and allow to rest under a dry tea towel for 15 minutes.

Shape each small piece of dough into a tight ball (see page 12) and place them on the prepared baking sheets. Cover with a dry tea towel and allow to rest for 45 minutes.

Preheat the oven to 220°C (425°F) Gas 7.

Flatten the buns slightly with your hand before popping them in the preheated oven and baking them for 20 minutes. Remove from the oven and allow to cool completely on a wire rack. Eat sparingly if you can!

Bollo de Hornasso   Gibraltar

The cooking of Gibraltar is a blend of North African, Spanish and English. Sound original? It certainly is. For such a tiny place, there is plenty of original food and Bollo de Hornasso is one thing you will only find there. The original Bollo de Hornazo is a kind of meat pie from Spain and heaven only knows how it transmogrified from that into a sweet bread that is popular at Easter and Christmas. If you know, let us know!

400 g/3 cups plain/
 all-purpose white
 wheat flour
2 g/1 teaspoon instant
 yeast, 4 g/1¼
 teaspoons dry yeast, or
 8 g/0.28 oz fresh yeast
75 g/⅓ cup sugar
250 g/1 cup milk, heated
 up to just below boiling
 point, then cooled to
 room temperature
8 g/2 teaspoons salt
2 tablespoons crushed
 anise seeds or 1
 teaspoon ground anise
50 g/3 tablespoons lard,
 at room temperature

Glaze
1 egg
1 tablespoon water
pinch of salt
pinch of sugar

Topping
flaked/slivered almonds
hundreds and thousands/
 sprinkles, chopped
 candied peel and/or fruit
 (optional)
sugar

*prepared baking sheets
 (see page 9)*

Makes 8 buns

Put the flour into a big mixing bowl and make a well. Sprinkle the yeast and sugar into the well and pour over the cooled milk. Flick some flour over the well to close it and cover it with a tea towel. Allow to rest for 1 hour.

Add the salt, anise and lard and bring the ingredients together in the bowl. Turn the dough out onto the counter and knead it well for 10 minutes. It's a sticky dough but don't add more flour. Put it back in the bowl, cover and allow to rest for 2 hours.

Pull the dough out onto a lightly floured surface.

(Continued overleaf.)

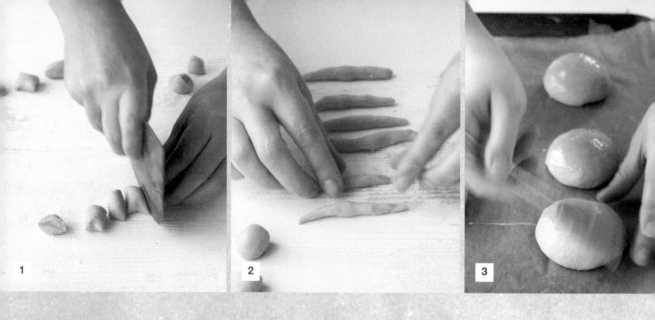

Shaping

Divide the dough into 8 equal portions and then pinch a 20 g/¾ oz blob of dough off each portion. Pop the little blobs of dough all together in a bowl (you can just pop them all in, you will measure and divide them later) and cover them with clingfilm/plastic wrap so they don't dry out.

Roll the bigger pieces of dough into tight balls (see page 12). Place the dough on a prepared baking sheet, cover with a dry tea towel and allow to rest for 40 minutes.

Preheat the oven to 220°C (425°F) Gas 7.

Return to the dough in the bowl. Merge it together and then take it out onto an unfloured surface and divide it into 3 equal pieces. Divide the first of the 3 pieces into 8 small bits and roll these into little balls. [1] Set them aside for the moment.

Divide the second of the 3 pieces into 8 pieces and roll these out into skinny little sausages about 8 cm/ 3¼ inches long. [2] Set them aside for the moment.

Divide the third of the 3 pieces into 8 pieces and roll these out into more skinny little sausages around 8 cm/3¼ inches long. Set them aside for the moment.

You now have 8 little balls and 16 little sausages.

Beat together the ingredients for the glaze and brush each bun with the glaze. [3]

Stick the tiny balls at the very top, in the centre, of each bun. Drape the dough sausages over the top of the buns to form an X, sticking them gently to the surface of the bun and on either side of the little balls on top in an effort to keep everything upright. [4, 5] Carefully brush the newly-applied dough with the glaze as well.

118 occasional buns

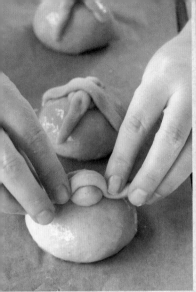 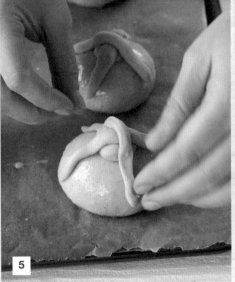 

5

6

Stick the almonds (hundreds and thousands/ sprinkles, candied fruit, etc., if you are using them) to the sides of the buns in between the dough sausages, and then sprinkle sugar over the top. [6]

Pop the buns in the preheated oven and bake for 20 minutes. Check them a few minutes before they are due to be done to make sure they are not burning. If they are too brown, cover them with aluminium foil or baking parchment.

Remove from the oven and allow them to cool completely on a wire rack.

Gibraltarian cooking is a glorious melting pot of traditional Spanish, Italian, English and North African cuisine. Dinner could include a rich fish soup, followed by an exotically spiced lamb dish and finished off with a Victoria sponge! Gibraltarian bread, however, has its roots firmly in Italy and Spain.

Pogácsa Hungary

I have a Hungarian friend called Gabor whose grandmothers are legends. They know the answer to every question, can make anything, and they provided this recipe for Pogácsa, which is a delicious Hungarian bun. A little mouthful of love.

3 tablespoons water
1.25 g/¾ teaspoon instant yeast, 2.5 g/1 teaspoon dry yeast, or 5 g/0.17 oz fresh yeast
250 g/2 cups plain/ all-purpose white wheat flour
5 g/1¼ teaspoons salt
200 g/13 tablespoons butter, cubed
1 egg yolk
100 g/6 tablespoons sour cream
1 tablespoon rum (optional)

Topping
1 egg white, beaten gently
125 g/1 generous cup grated hard cheese, such as gruyere or emmenthal (ie. not greasy, and one that melts well)
paprika (optional)

prepared baking sheets (see page 9)
round cookie cutter

Makes 20 buns

Put the water into a little bowl and sprinkle the yeast on top. Leave it while you deal with the flour and the butter. Put the flour into a big bowl and add the salt. Mix well. Add the butter and rub it into the flour with your fingers so that it becomes small crumbs. Then add the egg yolk, sour cream and yeast and water mixture (and rum if you are using it) and bring it together in the bowl. Make sure everything is mixed together well but treat it gently and don't over-knead it.

Cover the dough and allow it to rest for 2 hours at room temperature or all day/ overnight in the fridge. It won't rise much, it's really just resting.

Pull the dough out onto an unfloured surface and knead it for a minute or two. A scraper helps. Don't add more flour even though it's sticky.

Preheat the oven to 200°C (400°F) Gas 6.

Shaping

Flour the counter and a rolling pin and roll the dough to a thickness of 1 cm/½ inch. Brush with the egg white and sprinkle with the cheese and paprika, if you are using it. Cut the dough into small circles with a round cookie cutter or into squares with a knife. The shapes should be no more than 2 cm/¾ inch in diameter. Place each one on a prepared baking sheet. [1, 2]

Bake in the preheated oven for 30 minutes until they are golden brown. Remove from the oven and allow to cool completely on a wire rack before you eat them. Easy, impressive and impossibly moreish. Serve as an appetizer.

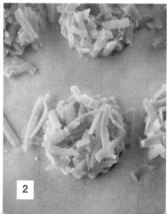

Tootmanik s Gotovo Testo Bulgaria

A few years ago when I was wandering around the world in my other life as a strategy consultant, the team and I kept getting taken out for Italian food. Don't get me wrong, I love Italian food but we were in Poland, the Czech Republic, Romania and Greece! Every night for about two weeks we ate Italian food because nobody would take us out for local fare. In Bulgaria, much to our delight, we were taken out for Bulgarian food and it was memorably delicious. Especially the bread. Cheesy, bakey yum yums. Need I say more?

450 g/3⅔ cups plain/
   all-purpose white
   wheat flour
2 g/1⅛ teaspoons instant
   yeast, 4.5 g/1½
   teaspoons dry yeast, or
   9 g/0.3 oz fresh yeast
250 g/1 cup milk, heated
   up to just below boiling
   point, then cooled to
   room temperature
9 g/2¼ teaspoons salt
100 g/6½ tablespoons
   butter

Filling
1 egg
250 g/8 oz feta cheese,
   crumbled into little
   pieces
50 g/3 tablespoons butter,
   melted and cooled
paprika, freshly ground
   pepper or chopped
   fresh herbs of your
   choice (optional)

Glaze
1 egg
1 teaspoon water

Decoration
sprinkle of paprika
   (optional)

baking pan 12 x 12 cm/
   4½ x 4½ inches and at
   least 5 cm/2 inches deep,
   greased and lined

Makes 12 large or 24
   small buns

Put the flour into a bowl and make a well. Sprinkle the yeast in the well and pour on the milk. Close the well by flicking flour on the surface of the milk and allow it to rest for 1 hour.

Add the salt and gather everything into a ball in the bowl. Turn it out on the counter and knead for 10 minutes. Add the butter and knead for another 10 minutes. Pop the dough back in the bowl, cover and allow to rest for 2 hours.

Mix the egg together with the feta cheese in a bowl. Melt the butter and allow it to cool.

Pull the dough out of the bowl onto an unfloured surface.

(Continued overleaf.)

Bulgarian bread is simply astonishing for its quality and variety and for the fact that it is still part of both daily and yearly life for everyone you talk to. Fresh bread – wheat or rye, plain or spicy, made with buttermilk or the delicious Bulgarian yogurt – is baked and bought daily, and sweet breads and buns mark rites of passage as well as the calendar year.

Shaping

Shape the dough into a tight sausage (see page 11). Cut it into 9 equal pieces. Lightly flour the top of each piece and allow to rest for 15 minutes under a dry tea towel.

Take out one piece and, on a floury surface, roll it into a rectangle about 10 x 10 cm/4 x 4 inches. [1] Brush it with the melted butter.

Take out another piece, roll it into a rectangle the same size as before, place it on the first piece and brush it with melted butter.

Take out a third piece, roll it into a rectangle the same size as before and place it on the stack. Don't brush it! [2]

Using a rolling pin, roll the stack of dough into a rectangle the size of your baking pan and lift it up (you can roll it around your rolling pin if that is easier) and place it in the prepared baking pan. [3]

2

3

Brush it with melted butter and spread over half the feta cheese mixture and any optional toppings. [4]

Repeat with the next 3 pieces of dough, and place that stack on top of the first stack. Brush this with melted butter and spread it with the other half of the feta cheese mixture and some more optional toppings.

Repeat with the final 3 pieces of dough, and place that stack on top of the dough in the pan.

With your hands, push down all around the outside edge of the stack of dough – between the dough and the pan – so that you seal in the cheese. Really pull down the very top layer of the bread and stick it well on or even under the rest of the dough. If you don't do this, it has a habit of springing free and looking like a kind of hat on top of the dough (you'll know if you do this, it's rather beautiful in its own way).

Cover with a dry tea towel and allow to rest for 1 hour.

Preheat the oven to 230°C (450°F) Gas 8.

Before baking, brush the top of the dough with melted butter and sprinkle some paprika on it if you like. [5] Pop the pan in the preheated oven and immediately turn the oven down to 200°C (400°F) Gas 6. Bake for 35 minutes.

Remove from the oven. Transfer carefully to a wire rack (inverting it onto a wire rack works well) and allow it to cool down a bit. When it is still warm (not hot), cut it into squares and eat it up alongside a salad or some soup for a wonderful, tasty meal.

2 eggs, beaten
100 g/6½ tablespoons milk,
    heated up to just below boiling
    point, then cooled to room
    temperature
100 g/6½ tablespoons butter,
    melted and allowed to cool
    slightly
1 teaspoon whiskey or brandy
½ teaspoon vanilla extract
500 g/4 cups plain/all-purpose
    white wheat flour
2.5 g/1¼ teaspoons instant yeast,
    5 g/1¾ teaspoons dry yeast, or
    10 g/0.35 oz fresh yeast
100 g/½ cup sugar
100 g/6½ tablespoons water
10 g/2½ teaspoons salt
1 teaspoon ground mahlab (see
    Sfoof ingredients, page 49)

Glaze
1 egg
1 tablespoon water
pinch of salt
pinch of sugar

Decoration
sesame seeds, sugar sprinkles,
    chocolate chips, pomegranate
    seeds or raisins

prepared baking sheets (see page 9)

Makes 16 buns

Chorek Armenia

Chorek is a sweet bun that is made to celebrate Easter. It comes in many different shapes – snail shells, something that looks a bit like a cottage loaf, and even little people. It is rich and buttery and gets its intriguing aroma and flavour from ground mahlab.

Beat the eggs thoroughly in a jug. In a big bowl, beat together the milk, melted butter, whiskey or brandy and vanilla extract. Gradually add in the eggs, beating the whole time to make something like a custard. Cover and allow to cool.

Put the flour in a big mixing bowl and make a well. Sprinkle the yeast and sugar into the well and pour in the water. Close the well by flicking some of the flour over the surface of the water. Cover the bowl and allow to rest for 1 hour.

Sprinkle the salt around the edge of the flour, add the mahlab and then add the milk and egg mixture. Bring everything together into a ball in the bowl. Turn the ball out onto the counter and knead well for 10 minutes.

Put the dough back in the bowl and allow it to rest, covered, for 2 hours.

Scrape the dough out gently onto an unfloured surface. It will be very soft but don't add flour.

Shaping
Divide the dough into 16 equal portions. Alternatively, if you want to make families, it is fun to have some large and some small pieces. Flour your hands and shape all the portions into tight balls (see page 12). Flour the tops and allow them to rest under a dry tea towel for 15 minutes.

To make snail shells: roll each ball into a sausage and then curl the sausage around itself to make a snail shell. [1]

To make cottage loaves: use a sharp knife to carve a little circle on top of each bun. Pinch the bit of dough in the circle to make a little ball on the top.

To make people: gently flatten the dough balls into rectangles about 2 cm/¾ inch thick and, using a knife or a scraper, make little people by following the instructions given for Grittibanz (pages 102–103).

Place each shape on the prepared baking sheet and cover them with a dry tea towel. Allow to rest for 1 hour.

Preheat the oven to 200°C (400°F) Gas 6.

Beat together the ingredients for the glaze and brush each bun with the glaze. Decorate the buns as you like and pop them in the preheated oven for 20 minutes.

Remove from the oven and allow them to cool completely on a wire rack before eating.

Sfeeha Syria

Sfeeha are little meat buns. They come from the Middle East and, as ever, there are many different recipes. This one is from Syria and the topping to the delicious bun base is a simple minced lamb stew. Like a lamb pizza. Only better.

600 g/4½ cups strong white (bread) flour
300 g/1¼ cups water
10 g/2 teaspoons olive oil
3 g/1½ teaspoons instant yeast, 6 g/2 teaspoons dry yeast, or 12 g/0.42 oz fresh yeast
12 g/1 tablespoon salt

Topping

4 tablespoons olive oil
200 g/6½ oz minced lamb
1 small onion, finely diced
½ green pepper, deseeded and finely diced
50 g/⅓ cup pine nuts
1 large tomato, deseeded and chopped
grated zest and juice of ½ lemon
a handful of chopped fresh parsley
½ teaspoon cayenne pepper
½ teaspoon ground cinnamon
½ teaspoon ground cumin
salt and pepper

big frying pan
prepared baking sheets (see page 9)

Makes 10 buns

1

If you are using instant or fresh yeast, put the flour into a big bowl and add all the other ingredients. Mix them together into a big ball and then turn this out onto the counter. Knead the dough well for 10 minutes.

If you are using dry yeast, put the flour into a big bowl and make a well. Sprinkle the yeast into the well and add the water. Cover and allow to rest for 15 minutes. A beige sludge may or may not form on the top of the water. Don't worry about it. As long as the yeast is fully dissolved it will work. After 15 minutes, add all the other ingredients. Mix them together into a big ball and then turn this out onto the counter. Knead the dough well for 10 minutes.

Pop the dough back in the bowl, cover and allow to rest for 2 hours.

For the topping, put 2 tablespoons of the oil in a big frying pan and add the minced lamb. Brown until thoroughly cooked and remove it with a slotted spoon to drain away the fat. Clean out the pan with kitchen paper/paper towels and return it to the heat.

Put the remaining oil in the pan and add the onion. Sweat this gently with the lid on for 5–6 minutes. Add the green pepper, pine nuts, tomato and lemon zest and juice and cook for another 5 minutes with the lid off. Add the lamb, parsley, spices and seasoning and stir it all around. Take it off the heat, cover and allow to cool completely.

Pull the dough out of the bowl onto an unfloured surface.

Shaping

Divide the dough into 10 equal portions and shape each portion into a tight ball (see page 12). Place each ball onto a floured surface and allow to rest for 30 minutes.

Take a ball of dough and press it down gently to double its size. Make a wide, shallow indentation in it (use the end of a rolling pin, the back of a spoon or just your fingers). [1] Fill the indentation with the lamb stew. If you are terrible at 'portion control' (like me) make the indentation in all 10 balls of dough and then top them so they all get an equal amount of topping. Place each sfeeha on a prepared baking sheet and allow to rest for 45 minutes, covered with a dry tea towel.

Preheat the oven to 220°C (425°F) Gas 7.

Pop the sfeeha in the preheated oven and bake for 20 minutes. Remove from the oven and allow them to cool slightly on a wire rack before eating.

600 g/4¾ cups plain/all-purpose
  white wheat flour
3 g/1½ teaspoons instant yeast,
  6 g/2 teaspoons dry yeast, or
  12 g/0.42 oz fresh yeast
100 g/½ cup sugar
225 g/1 scant cup milk, heated up
  to boiling point, then cooled to
  room temperature
2 eggs
½ teaspoon rose water
½ teaspoon orange blossom water
½ teaspoon ground cardamom
½ teaspoon ground mahlab (see
  Sfoof ingredients, page 49)
12 g/1 tablespoon salt
50 g/3 tablespoons butter, melted
  and allowed to cool

Glaze
1 egg
1 tablespoon water
pinch of salt
pinch sugar

Decoration
sesame seeds

prepared baking sheets (see page 9)

Makes 12 buns

1

Shubbak el-Habayeb Iraq

*The wonderful name of these beautiful buns is translated as
The Lover's Window, which kind of makes me want to cry every
time I think about it – it's just so lovely! I would love to know
who named it and whether they ever found their true love.*

Put the flour into a bowl and make a well. Sprinkle the yeast and sugar in the
well and pour over the milk. Close the well by flicking some flour on top of
the milk. Cover the bowl and allow it to rest for 1 hour.

Add the rest of the ingredients, except the butter, into the bowl and
gather them into a ball. Turn the dough out onto the counter and knead for
10 minutes. Add the butter and knead for another 10 minutes. Pop the
dough back into the bowl, cover and allow to rest for 2 hours.

Pull the dough out gently onto an unfloured surface.

Shaping

Divide the dough into 12 equal portions. Shape each portion into a tight ball
(see page 12). Allow to rest under a dry tea towel for 15 minutes.

Take each ball and roll it with a rolling pin into a little square about 1 cm/
½ inch thick. Make a short vertical slit in each quadrant of the dough square.
Make sure there is dough between each slit and open the slit with your
fingers so it does not close up while the dough is rising. [1]

Transfer each portion of dough with your scraper onto a prepared baking
sheet. Flour the tops lightly and cover with a dry tea towel. Allow to rest for
1 hour.

Preheat the oven to 220°C (425°F) Gas 7.

Re-open the cuts if they have sealed themselves shut while the dough has
been resting. Beat together the ingredients for the glaze and brush the buns
with it. Sprinkle the sesame seeds on the top and pop the buns in the
preheated oven for 15 minutes.

Remove from the oven and allow to cool on a wire rack, before eating
them while you think of your true love.

Krachel Morocco

This lovely, fragrant bun – or at least a version of it – is enjoyed with cups of fresh mint tea all over the Middle East and North Africa at any time of day. You can leave out the nuts if you like but do look for some orange blossom water as it lifts the buns amazingly. You can usually get it at a chemist and failing that, any Middle Eastern or North African shop will stock it.

50 g/3 tablespoons honey
200 g/¾ cup milk
600 g/4¾ cups plain/
   all-purpose white
   wheat flour
3 g/1½ teaspoons instant
   yeast, 6 g/2 teaspoons
   dry yeast, or 12 g/
   0.42 oz fresh yeast
12 g/1 tablespoon salt
100 g/6½ tablespoons
   butter, melted and
   allowed to cool slightly
2 teaspoons whole
   aniseeds
2 eggs
2 teaspoons orange
   blossom water
200 g/1⅓ cups pistachio
   nuts/kernels

Glaze
1 egg
1 tablespoon water
pinch of salt
pinch of sugar

*prepared baking sheets
   (see page 9)*

Makes 16 buns

Put the honey into the milk and heat it up to boiling point, stirring all the time to dissolve the honey. Allow to cool right down.

Put the flour in a big bowl and make a well. Sprinkle the yeast into the well and pour over the milk mixture. Flick some of the flour on top of the milk to close the well and allow to rest for 1 hour.

Sprinkle the salt around the edge of the flour and add all the other ingredients, except the pistachio nuts, into the bowl. Gather them together into a big ball and then turn the dough out onto the counter. Knead well for 10 minutes and then pop it back in the bowl. Cover and allow to rest for 30 minutes.

While you wait, toast the pistachio nuts/kernels in a dry frying pan being careful not to burn them. When they are lightly toasted, and you can smell them, remove from the heat and coarsely chop them with a knife. A machine grinds them too finely.

Add the nuts to the dough, squashing them into the dough to distribute them evenly. Don't worry about the dough, it will recover. Cover and allow to rest for 1½ hours. Pull the dough out onto an unfloured surface.

Shaping

Divide the dough into 16 equal portions and allow to rest under a dry tea towel for 15 minutes.

Shape each portion of dough into a tight ball (see page 12) and place them on the prepared baking sheets. Cover and allow to rest for 45 minutes.

Preheat the oven to 220°C (425°F) Gas 7.

Beat together the ingredients for the glaze and brush it on the buns. Pop them in the preheated oven for 15 minutes.

Remove from the oven and allow to cool completely on a wire rack.

Chocolate Sticks South Africa

In my first book there is a description of a bread safari in the Western Cape. One of the amazing bakeries in that lovely region of the world is De Oude Bank Bakkerij in Stellenbosch. The bread is fantastic and these chocolate sticks are super fantastic. I have made the recipe up because I forgot to ask for it and I think the result is close to the real thing.

Predough
100 g/scant ½ cup warm water
150 g/1 heaping cup plain/all-purpose white wheat flour
pinch of yeast (any kind will do)

Dough
300 g/2⅓ cups plain/all-purpose white wheat flour
50 g/¼ cup sugar
1 g/½ teaspoon instant yeast, 2 g/1 scant teaspoon dry yeast, or 4 g/0.15 oz fresh yeast
200 g/¾ cup milk, heated up to boiling point, then cooled to room temperature
5 g/1¼ teaspoons salt

Filling
50 g/3 tablespoons butter, melted and allowed to cool slightly
200 g/6½ oz chocolate chips or chunks

Glaze
1 egg
1 tablespoon water
pinch of salt
pinch of sugar

prepared baking sheets (see page 9)

Makes lots depending on how big you make them

Day One: making a predough
Mix together the water, flour and yeast in a bowl until they are well blended. Cover with clingfilm/plastic wrap and allow to sit on the counter for 12–48 hours. The longer it sits the tastier it will be.

Day Two: making the dough
Put the flour into a big bowl and make a well. Sprinkle the sugar and yeast into the well and pour in the milk. Flick some flour over the milk to close the well and allow to rest for 1 hour. Add the salt and the predough from the night before. Bring it all together in a ball in the bowl. Pull it out onto the counter and knead well for 10 minutes.

Lightly flour a surface on which you can cut (you will see why later) and roll out the dough to a thickness of 5 mm/¼ inch. Brush the top with some of the melted butter for the filling and cover it with clingfilm/plastic wrap. Allow to rest for 2 hours.

Shaping
Remove the clingfilm/plastic wrap. Scatter a third of the chocolate chips over the dough. Fold the left edge to the middle and fold the right edge in to meet it. Flour around the dough. Roll the dough flat again, brush some more melted butter on it and scatter over another third of the chocolate chips. Fold the dough as above and flour around it. Roll the dough flat again, brush some more melted butter on it and scatter over the final third of the chocolate chips. Fold the dough as above, lightly flour it and flip it over so the floury side is down. Flour the top, cover with a tea towel and allow to rest for 45 minutes.

Preheat the oven to 230°C (450°F) Gas 8.

Beat together the ingredients for the glaze and brush it over the dough. Using a knife, scraper or pizza cutter, cut the dough into strips about 2.5 cm/1 inch wide. If the strips are too long, cut them in half. Place the strips on the prepared baking sheets. Pop them in the preheated oven for 15 minutes.

Remove from the oven. It is hard to resist eating these warm and they are wonderful dipped into a cup of coffee or hot chocolate.

Scalded dough

50 g/scant ½ cup plain/
   all-purpose white
   wheat flour
75 g/⅓ cup boiling water

Dough

350 g/2¾ cups plain/
   all-purpose white
   wheat flour
50 g/¼ cup sugar
2 g/1 teaspoon instant
   yeast, 3.5 g/1⅛
   teaspoons dry yeast, or
   7 g/0.25 oz fresh yeast
125 g/½ cup milk, heated
   up to just below boiling
   point, then cooled to
   room temperature
7 g/1½ teaspoons salt
1 egg
50 g/3 tablespoons butter

Filling

30 g/2 tablespoons butter,
   at room temperature
30 g/4 tablespoons icing/
   confectioners' sugar
1 egg yolk (save the white
   for glazing)
60 g/½ cup unsweetened,
   desiccated/shredded
   coconut

Glaze

1 egg white
1 tablespoon water
pinch of salt
pinch of sugar

Decoration

sesame seeds

*prepared baking sheets
   (see page 9)*

Makes 10 buns

Coconut Buns China

*In general, Chinese sweets are one of those things that you either
love or you hate. I am happy to say that these buns are the exception to
the rule because they are just universally delicious (if you like coconut)
and they are wonderful buns to nibble on while you drink a cup of
piping hot Chinese tea.*

Making the scalded dough

Put the flour into a little bowl and pour over the boiling water. Stir well, cover and
allow to cool completely.

Making the dough

Put the flour into a big bowl and make a well. Sprinkle the sugar and yeast into the
well and pour over the milk. Close the well by flicking some flour on top of the milk,
cover and allow to rest for 1 hour.

Sprinkle the salt around the edge of the flour, add the egg and scalded dough and
bring the dough together into a ball in the bowl. Turn out onto the counter and knead
well for 10 minutes. Add the butter and knead for a further 10 minutes.

Pop it back into the bowl and cover it. Allow to rest for 2 hours. In that time, make
the filling by beating all the ingredients together. Cover and set aside until you need it.

Pull the dough out gently onto an unfloured surface.

Shaping

Divide the dough into 10 equal portions. Shape each portion into a tight ball (see
page 12). Allow to rest for 15 minutes under a dry tea towel.

Flour the counter and, using a floury rolling pin, flatten a piece of dough into a long,
thin oblong. Spread a blob of the filling over the oblong.

Roll the oblong up into a sausage, give it a quarter of a turn and flatten it again
with the rolling pin. Roll it up for a second time and shape it into a tight ball (see page
12). Place on a prepared baking sheet. Repeat with the remaining balls of dough and
filling, cover and allow to rest for 45 minutes.

Preheat the oven to 220°C (425°F) Gas 7.

Before you bake the buns, beat together the ingredients for the glaze, brush the
buns with the glaze and sprinkle sesame seeds on top. Bake in the preheated oven
for 15 minutes. Remove from the oven and allow to cool completely on a wire rack
before you eat them. I warn you, these are delicious and it is hard to have just one.
So, invite some friends round.

Scalded dough

70 g/½ cup plain/
 all-purpose white
 wheat flour
50 g/¼ cup boiling water

Dough

350 g/2¾ cups plain/
 all-purpose white
 wheat flour
2 g/1 teaspoon instant
 yeast, 4 g/1¼
 teaspoons dry yeast, or
 8 g/0.28 oz fresh yeast
70 g/⅓ cup sugar
125 g/½ cup milk, heated
 up to boiling point, then
 cooled to room
 temperature
8 g/2 teaspoons salt
1 egg
60 g/5 tablespoons butter,
 at room temperature,
 cubed

Topping

40 g/2 tablespoons plus
 2 teaspoons butter, at
 room temperature
50 g/¼ cup sugar
1 egg
125 g/1 cup plain/
 all-purpose white
 wheat flour
¼ teaspoon baking
 powder
a splash of milk

Glaze

1 egg
1 tablespoon water
pinch of salt
pinch of sugar

*prepared baking sheets
 (see page 9)*

Makes 12 buns

Buoluo Bao Hong Kong

Buoluo Bao translates as 'pineapple buns' and they are a bit of a cult favourite in Hong Kong. They do not contain pineapple! However, the tops are sometimes scored into a diamond pattern so they kind of look like the skin of a pineapple.

Making the scalded dough

Put the flour into a little bowl and pour over the boiling water. Stir with a spoon to mix the flour and water completely. Cover and set aside to cool.

Making the dough

Put the flour into a big mixing bowl and make a well. Sprinkle the yeast and sugar into the well and pour over the milk. Flick some flour over the milk to close the well and cover it with a tea towel. Allow to rest for 1 hour.

Add the salt, egg and scalded dough (break it up into bits as this makes it easier to incorporate it) and bring the ingredients together in the bowl. Turn the dough out on the counter and knead it well for 10 minutes. Add the butter and knead again for 10 minutes. Put it back in the bowl, cover and allow to rest for 2 hours.

Beat together all the ingredients for the topping and set aside.

Pull the dough out onto an unfloured surface.

Shaping

Divide the dough into 12 equal portions. Roll each portion into a tight ball (see page 12). Place the tight balls on a prepared baking sheet. Cover with a tea towel and allow to rest for 30 minutes.

Take the topping and divide it into 12 equal blobs. Keep a little bowl of water to hand to wet your hands because the topping is very sticky.

Topping

With wet hands, take a blob of topping and roll it between your palms into a little ball. Stretch the ball out into a disc about 5 mm/¼ inch thick and, thus, about the size of the top of a bun.

Place the disc on top of a bun and press down gently to seal it on and to flatten the bun to a height of about 2 cm/¾ inch. Repeat this for all the other buns. Leave the topped buns to rest, uncovered, for about 15 minutes.

Preheat the oven to 220°C (425°F) Gas 7.

Just before you bake the buns, flatten them again to about 2 cm/¾ inch high and, if you wish, score their tops in a diamond pattern so they look a bit like the skin of a pineapple. Beat together the ingredients for the glaze and brush it on. Pop the buns in the preheated oven and bake for 15 minutes. Check when there are a few minutes to go and cover with aluminium foil or baking parchment if they are getting too brown. Cool completely on a wire rack.

Anpan/Jampan Japan

Dainty little sweets to eat while you drink tea are a hallmark of Japanese culture. Whilst many are made with glutinous rice paste wrapped around a sesame, sweet potato or red bean paste filling, anpan are buns made from wheat flour and baked in the oven. They are not super sweet and the red bean paste takes a little getting used to. If it's not for you, stuff the buns with jam.

For the scalded dough
50 g/⅓ cup plain/
   all-purpose white
   wheat flour
75 g/⅓ cup boiling water

Dough
350 g/2¾ cups plain/
   all-purpose white
   wheat flour
50 g/¼ cup sugar
2 g/1 teaspoon instant
   yeast, 3.5 g/1⅛
   teaspoons dry yeast, or
   7 g/0.25 oz fresh yeast
150 g/scant ⅔ cup milk,
   heated up to just below
   boiling point, then
   cooled to room
   temperature
7 g/1¾ teaspoons salt
1 egg
50 g/3 tablespoons butter

Filling
200 g/¾ cup red bean
   paste or jam

Glaze
1 egg white
1 tablespoon water
pinch of salt
pinch of sugar

*prepared baking sheets
   (see page 9)*

Makes 20 dainty little
   buns

Making the scalded dough

Put the flour into a little bowl and pour over the boiling water. Stir well, cover and allow to cool completely.

Making the dough

Put the flour into a big bowl and make a well. Sprinkle the sugar and yeast into the well and pour over the milk. Close the well by flicking some flour on top of the milk and cover it with a dry tea towel. Allow to rest for 1 hour.

Sprinkle the salt around the edge of the flour, add the egg and the scalded dough and bring the dough together into a ball in the bowl. Turn it out on the counter and knead well for 10 minutes. Add the butter and knead for a further 10 minutes. The dough is quite stiff.

Pop it back into the bowl and cover it. Allow it to rest for 2 hours.

Pull the dough out onto an unfloured surface.

Shaping

Divide the dough into 4 equal portions. Shape each portion into a tight sausage (see page 11). Divide each sausage into 5 equal portions and allow to rest for 15 minutes under a dry tea towel.

Take a piece of dough and flatten it with your hand or a rolling pin into a disc. Pop a little blob of red bean paste (or jam) in the centre and bring the edges of the dough up and around it like a parcel. Pinch the edges tightly to seal them (see page 15 'to fill and shape a ball'). Place the parcel seam-side-down on a prepared baking sheet. Repeat with the remaining dough portions and paste. Cover with a dry tea towel and allow to rest for 45 minutes.

Preheat the oven to 220°C (425°F) Gas 7.

To glaze, mix together the egg white, water, salt and sugar and brush it on the buns. Pop them in the preheated oven for 15 minutes. Remove from the oven and allow cool to completely before you eat them.

Peperechas El Salvador

Peperechas is actually an El Salvadorian slang word for prostitutes. I had to include that little piece of knowledge otherwise you would all be writing to me to tell me I had neglected it. Sorry if I offended anyone! These little buns are filled, in quite a cunning way, with jam and mild cheese which is a winning combination at breakfast, or any time of the day.

Dough

250 g/2 cups plain/
  all-purpose white
  wheat flour
1.25 g/¾ teaspoon instant
  yeast, 2.5 g/1 teaspoon
  dry yeast, or 5 g/0.17 oz
  fresh yeast
70 g/⅓ cup sugar
125 g/½ cup water
5 g/1¼ teaspoons salt
80 g/5½ tablespoons
  butter, at room
  temperature, cubed

Filling

4 tablespoons jam of your
  choice
125 g/4 oz panela cheese
  (you can substitute
  mozzarella)

Glaze

1 egg
1 tablespoon water
pinch of salt
pinch of sugar

Topping

sugar (dye it red with a few
  drops of red food
  colouring if you want to
  be traditional)

*prepared baking sheets
  (see page 9)*

Makes 12 buns

Making a predough

Put the flour into a big mixing bowl and make a well. Sprinkle the yeast and sugar into the well and pour over the water. Flick some flour over the water to close the well and cover with a tea towel. Allow to rest for 1 hour.

Making the dough

Add the salt to the predough and bring the ingredients together in the bowl. Turn the dough out onto the counter and knead it well for 10 minutes. It will be quite stiff so do your best. Then add the butter and knead for another 10 minutes. The dough will be very soft and sticky at this point but don't be tempted to add any more flour. Use a scraper to help you knead. Put the dough back in the bowl, cover and allow to rest for 2 hours.

Pull the dough out onto a floured surface.

Shaping

Divide the dough into 2 equal portions. It will be very soft, but don't worry. Flour the top of the dough and, using a floury rolling pin, gently roll out one of the pieces into a rectangle or a square about 5 mm/¼ inch thick. Transfer carefully to the prepared baking sheet. Spread the jam on the flattened dough and sprinkle the cheese on the top.

Roll out the second piece of dough to match the first one and carefully lay it on top of the first so that you have made a sandwich with the jam and cheese in the middle. Cover with a dry tea towel and allow to rest for 45 minutes.

Preheat the oven to 220°C (425°F) Gas 7.

Beat all the ingredients for the glaze together and brush it on top of the dough. Sprinkle sugar liberally over the dough. Using a wet scraper or a wet knife (this makes it easier), cut the dough into 12 equal squares/rectangles/triangles – whatever you would like to do. Don't try to separate the pieces, do make the cuts all the way through the dough to the bottom. You will pull them apart when they are baked.

Pop the buns into the preheated oven for 20 minutes. Remove them from the oven and, using a palette knife, separate the shapes and place them on a cooling rack. Don't bite into them hot: you will burn your tongue on the jam!

Niños Envueltos Mexico

Niños envueltos literally means 'wrapped up babies' and for that I love these buns. You see them all over Latin America and the Caribbean with both savoury (cheese, beans, pulled chicken or pork) and sweet fillings. The term can also be used to describe a stuffed and rolled roast or a fancy swirly sandwich. This is a fun bun – perfect for children's parties and lunchboxes.

300 g/2⅓ cups plain/
   all-purpose white
   wheat flour
50 g/3 tablespoons sugar
1.5 g/¾ teaspoon instant
   yeast, 3 g/1 teaspoon
   dry yeast, or 6 g/0.2 oz
   fresh yeast
200 g/¾ cup plus 1
   tablespoon milk, heated
   up to just below boiling
   point, then cooled to
   room temperature
6 g/1½ teaspoons salt
50 g/3 tablespoons butter

Filling
jam of your choice

Glaze
1 egg
1 tablespoon water
pinch of salt
pinch of sugar

*prepared baking sheets
  (see page 9)*

Makes 16 buns

Put the flour into a bowl and make a well. Sprinkle the sugar and yeast into the well and pour in the milk. Flick some flour on the surface of the milk to close the well and cover the bowl. Allow to rest for 1 hour.

Add the salt and mix the ingredients together into a ball in the bowl. Turn this out onto the counter and knead for 10 minutes. Add the butter and knead for a further 10 minutes.

Pop the dough back into the bowl and cover it. Allow to rest for 2 hours.

Pull the dough out onto a floured surface.

Shaping

Roll the dough into a rectangle about 20 x 15 cm/8 x 6 inches. Spread jam all over the dough and then roll it up tightly from the long edge, stretching it towards you slightly between rolls, into a tight sausage. Slice the sausage into slices about 1 cm/½ inch thick (see page 14). Place them on a prepared baking sheet, leaving a little space between them so they don't touch as they rise. Cover with a dry tea towel and allow to rest for 45 minutes.

Preheat the oven to 220°C (425°F) Gas 7.

Beat together all the ingredients for the glaze and brush the buns. Pop the buns in the preheated oven and bake them for 15–20 minutes. Check after 10 minutes and cover with foil or baking parchment if they are getting too brown. Allow them to cool completely on a wire rack before eating.

Predough

25 g/3 tablespoons plain/all-purpose white wheat flour
125 g/½ cup water

Filling

3–4 apples, peeled, cored and cut into small pieces
50 g/¼ cup brown sugar
½ teaspoon ground cinnamon
pinch each of ground cloves, nutmeg and salt
grated zest of 1 lemon
50 g/3 tablespoons butter

Dough

475 g/3¾ cups plain/all-purpose white wheat flour
50 g/¼ cup sugar
2.5 g/1¼ teaspoons instant yeast, 5 g/1¾ teaspoons dry yeast, or 10 g/0.35 oz fresh yeast
50 g/3 tablespoons milk, heated up to boiling point, then cooled to room temperature
150 g/scant ⅔ cup water
10 g/2½ teaspoons salt
1 egg
50 g/3 tablespoons butter

Glaze

1 egg
1 tablespoon water
pinch of salt
pinch of sugar

Decoration

ground cinnamon, to sprinkle

prepared baking sheets (see page 9)

Makes 16 buns

Apple Buns USA

The great thing about apples is that you can more or less get them all year round which means you can make these buns any time although, I confess, I love to eat them in the winter. They are warm and round and spicy and remind me of little russet apples which come out around Christmas time.

Day One: making a predough

Mix the flour and water together in a big bowl. Cover it with clingfilm/plastic wrap and allow to rest for 12–24 hours.

Place all the filling ingredients into a saucepan and simmer gently until the apples are soft. Add a tiny bit of water if the apples are sticking. Remove from the heat, cover and set aside until you need it.

Day Two: making the dough

Put the flour into the bowl with the predough and make a well. Sprinkle the sugar and yeast into the well and pour over the milk and water. Close the well by flicking some flour over the surface of the liquid. Cover and allow to rest for 1 hour.

Sprinkle the salt around the edge of the flour and add the egg and the predough. Mix the ingredients together to form a ball. Turn it out onto the counter and knead for 10 minutes. Add the butter and knead for another 10 minutes. Pop it back in the bowl and cover it. Allow to rest for 2 hours.

Pull the dough out gently onto an unfloured surface.

Shaping

Shape the dough into a tight sausage (see page 11). Divide the sausage into 16 equal portions and allow to rest under a dry tea towel for 15 minutes.

Lightly flour the counter. Take a piece of dough and stretch it out gently with your hands into a disc about 5 mm/¼ inch thick. Put a spoonful of the apple mixture in the centre of the disc and pull the edges up around the apple mixture. Press the edges together to seal them tightly and place the bun seam-side-down on a prepared baking sheet (see page15 'to fill and shape a ball'). Repeat with all the other portions of dough. Cover with a dry tea towel and allow to rest for 45 minutes.

Preheat the oven to 220°C (425°F) Gas 7.

Beat all the glaze ingredients together. Glaze the buns and sprinkle on some ground cinnamon before popping them into the preheated oven. Bake for 15 minutes. Remove from the oven and allow to cool completely on a wire rack before you bite into them.

Cornmeal Buns USA

Cornmeal (also known as polenta) makes an excellent addition to bread and buns. Using it without wheat flour you can bake lovely, gluten-free bread, and using it with wheat flour you can bake a wonderfully textured bread or bun that is surprisingly light and has a great flavour. These buns are delicious at breakfast with honey or jam, and equally satisfying with lunch or dinner.

For the cornmeal 'mush'
150 g/1 heaping cup coarsely ground cornmeal/polenta
30 g/2 tablespoons lard or butter
60 g/¼ cup honey or molasses
250 g/1 cup milk

Dough
500 g/3¾ cups strong white or wholemeal/whole-wheat (bread) flour
2.5 g/1¼ teaspoons instant yeast, 5 g/1¾ teaspoons dry yeast, or 10 g/0.35 oz fresh yeast
10 g/2½ teaspoons salt
150 g/scant ⅔ cup water

Glaze
1 egg
1 teaspoon water
pinch of salt
pinch of sugar

Decoration
a little cornmeal/polenta

prepared baking sheets (see page 9)

Makes 18 buns

For the cornmeal 'mush', put the cornmeal/polenta into a small bowl and add the lard or butter and the honey or molasses. Heat the milk to just below boiling point and then pour it over the contents of the bowl. Stir it around to melt the fat and mix everything up. Leave it to cool down completely.

For the dough, put the flour into a big mixing bowl.

If you are using instant or fresh yeast, simply sprinkle it into the bowl with the flour, add all of the remaining ingredients, including the cornmeal 'mush', and mix it together into a ball. Turn this out on the counter and knead well for 10 minutes.

If you are using dry yeast, make a well in the flour and sprinkle in the yeast. Add the water and allow it to rest for 15 minutes. A beige sludge may or may not form on the top. Don't worry about it. As long as the yeast is fully dissolved it will work. After 15 minutes, put in all the other ingredients including the cornmeal 'mush' and mix it together into a ball. Turn this out on the counter and knead well for 10 minutes.

Once done, pop the dough back in the bowl, cover and allow to rest for 2 hours.

Pull the dough out gently onto an unfloured surface.

Shaping
Divide the dough into 18 equal portions. Shape each of these into a tight ball (see page 12). Place on a prepared baking sheet. Cover with a dry tea towel and allow them to rest for 1 hour.

Preheat the oven to 220°C (425°F) Gas 7.

Just before you pop the buns in the oven, beat all the glaze ingredients together, brush the buns with the glaze and sprinkle some cornmeal/polenta over them.

Bake in the preheated oven for 20 minutes. Remove from the oven and allow to cool on a wire rack.

600 g/4¾ cups plain/all-purpose
  white wheat flour
3 g/1½ teaspoons instant yeast,
  6 g/2 teaspoons dry yeast, or
  12 g/0.42 oz fresh yeast
50 g/¼ cup sugar
225 g/1 cup milk, heated up to
  boiling point, then cooled to
  room temperature
12 g/1 tablespoon salt
2 eggs
2 teaspoons vanilla extract
50 g/3 tablespoons butter

For the deliciousness
100 g/½ cup brown sugar
2 tablespoons ground cinnamon
100 g/¾ cup chopped pecans
100 g/6½ tablespoons butter

baking pan with deep sides

Makes 24 small buns

Monkey Buns USA

*The origin of the name Monkey Buns (also called Monkey
Puzzle Bread, Sticky Bread, African Coffee Cake, Golden
Crown, Pinch-Me Cake, Bubble Loaf and Monkey Brains) is
uncertain. What is not uncertain is that it is delicious in almost
any form.*

Put the flour into a bowl and make a well. Sprinkle the yeast and sugar in the
well and pour over the milk. Flick some flour over the surface of the milk to
close the well and allow to rest for 1 hour.

Sprinkle the salt around the edge of the flour, add the eggs and vanilla
extract into the centre and bring everything together in the bowl. Turn the
dough out onto the counter and knead for 10 minutes. Add the butter and
knead for a further 10 minutes. Pop the dough back in the bowl and allow to
rest for 2 hours.

Turn the dough out onto an unfloured surface. It is sticky but try not to add
more flour. The stickiness is important as you will see later on.

Shaping

Divide the dough into 4 equal portions. Shape each portion into a tight
sausage (see page 11). Cut each sausage into 6 pieces and allow to rest
under a dry tea towel for 15 minutes.

Butter a baking pan with deep sides. Almost anything will do – but you
want to pile the buns on top of each other so use a deep cake pan rather
than a shallow roasting pan. Use a solid pan, not one with a removable
bottom because the butter tends to leak out and burn on the bottom of your
oven. Finally, remember the buns will rise, so pick a pan that is big enough so
that the buns do not come all the way over the top before they are baked.

Form each portion of dough into a tight ball (see page 12).

Mix the brown sugar and cinnamon together. Put 6 buns in the bottom of
the prepared pan and sprinkle a third of the cinnamon-sugar and a third of
the pecans over the dough. [1] Repeat until you have used up all the dough
balls, cinnamon-sugar and pecans. Cover and allow to rest for 45 minutes.

Preheat the oven to 200°C (400°F) Gas 6.

Before baking the buns, melt the butter and let it cool slightly. You want it
to be liquid but not boiling hot. Pour the melted butter evenly over the buns
and then pop them in the preheated oven and bake for 45 minutes. After
30 minutes, cover them with aluminium foil or baking parchment so they
don't get too brown. Remove from the oven. Allow to rest in the pan for
10 minutes before turning them out onto a plate (be careful of the delicious,
hot, melty butter mixture) and sharing them.

Autumnal Sticky Buns Canada

Sticky buns are a very Canadian thing and they come in many varieties (all of the sticky kind). One of the classic varieties, for example, is cinnamon buns, the recipe for which is in my first book. This sticky bun recipe, however, has a twist. Rather than milk or water for the liquid in the dough, you use puréed pumpkin (canned pumpkin is perfectly great) and if you cannot find that, you can always use puréed apple or pear. A great autumnal breakfast bun.

600 g/4¾ cups plain/
   all-purpose white
   wheat flour
3 g/1½ teaspoons instant
   yeast, 6 g/2 teaspoons
   dry yeast, or 12 g/
   0.42 oz fresh yeast
50 g/¼ cup sugar
75 g/scant ⅓ cup milk,
   heated up to boiling
   point, then cooled to
   room temperature
12 g/1 tablespoon salt
1 egg
350 g/scant 1½ cups
   pumpkin purée
50 g/3 tablespoons butter

Filling
50 g/3 tablespoons
   pumpkin purée
1 teaspoon each of
   ground cinnamon,
   nutmeg, ginger and
   allspice
50 g/¼ cup brown sugar
50 g/3 tablespoons butter,
   softened

Goo
100 g/6½ tablespoons
   butter, melted
100 g/½ cup brown sugar
75 g/⅓ cup milk or cream
100 g/¾ cup chopped
   pecans

large, deep roasting pan

Makes 16 buns

Put the flour into a big bowl and make a well. Sprinkle the yeast and sugar into the well and pour over the milk. Flick some flour on the surface of the milk to close the well. Allow to rest for 1 hour.

Sprinkle the salt around the edge of the flour and add the egg and the pumpkin purée. Gather everything into a ball and then turn it out onto the counter. Knead for 10 minutes. Add the butter and knead for another 10 minutes.

Pop it back in the bowl and allow it to rest for 2 hours.

Beat together the ingredients for the filling and set the mixture aside.

Mix together the ingredients for the goo and pour the mixture into a large, deep roasting pan about 30 x 20 cm/12 x 8 inches. Set aside.

Pull the dough out onto a floured surface.

Shaping
Roll the dough with a rolling pin into a rectangle about 40 x 20 cm/16 x 8 inches. Spread the filling evenly over the dough and then roll the rectangle up into a tight sausage from the long side. Slice the sausage into 16 equal pieces (see page 14). Place each piece, cut-side-up, in the baking pan on top of the goo. Snuggle them together if you have to in order to fit them all in. Cover and allow to rest for 45 minutes.

Preheat the oven to 200°C (400°F) Gas 6.

Pop the buns in the preheated oven and bake for 45 minutes. After 30 minutes, cover them with baking parchment or aluminium foil to prevent the tops getting too brown. When they are done, remove from the oven, place a large plate over the pan and carefully invert the buns onto the plate. Don't spill the hot goo! It's delicious and you don't want to waste it or burn yourself.

Allow to cool slightly before eating them.

Predough

225 g/1 cup really finely mashed potato

225 g/1 cup water in which the potatoes were boiled

125 g/1 cup plain/all-purpose white wheat flour

3 g/1½ teaspoons instant yeast, 6 g/2 teaspoons dry yeast, or 12 g/0.42 oz fresh yeast

Dough

225 g/1 cup plus 2 tablespoons sugar

200 g/¾ cup plus 1 tablespoon milk, heated up to boiling point, then cooled to room temperature

175 g/12 tablespoons butter, melted and allowed to cool slightly

3 eggs, beaten

6 g/1½ teaspoons salt

825 g/6¼ cups plain/all-purpose white wheat flour

To fry

1.5 litres/6 cups high 'smoke point' oil, such as peanut, safflower or rapeseed

Decoration

cinnamon sugar or maple syrup

Makes between 25–50 depending on how big you make them (smaller is better)

Fastnachts Canada

I could not decide which bun to put last in the book so I asked around. Of the many suggested the one that stuck was doughnuts, put forward by Joanna Carey and Al Instone. I adapted a recipe from a Canadian cookbook called 'Food That Really Schmecks' by Edna Staebler. It is a Mennonite recipe for Fastnachts eaten on Shrove Tuesday. Canadians eat more doughnuts per capita than any other nation, so I guess we eat these more than once a year. Join us – you won't regret it. They are fab.

Day One: making a predough

Put all the ingredients for the predough into a big mixing bowl and mix them well. Cover with clingfilm/plastic wrap and allow to rest overnight.

Day Two: making the dough

Add all the dough ingredients except the flour to the predough. Beat the mixture thoroughly and then add the flour, stirring constantly. The result is somewhere in between a very stiff batter and very loose dough. Do not add more flour. Cover and allow to rest for 2 hours.

(Continued overleaf.)

Shaping

Pour about half of the dough out onto a very floury counter and generously flour the top of the dough (there is a lot of dough, so just do half at a time). [1] The dough is very runny but don't worry about that, it's normal. Using a scraper, fold the left and then the right sides of the dough into the middle and then fold the top and the bottom of the dough into the middle, working as quickly as you can. [2] Flour the top again and flip the dough over. Using a scraper that you regularly dip in flour, cut the dough into squares no more than about 3 cm/1¼ inches across. [3]

Using a scraper to lift them, place each square on floured surface and snip a slash in all of them from one corner to another using scissors.

Flour them lightly and cover them with a dry tea towel. Repeat with the other half of the dough. Allow to rest for 1 hour.

Heat the oil in a large saucepan or deep fat fryer to 190°C (375°F). If you don't have a thermometer, test the temperature of the oil by dropping in a few breadcrumbs. If they drop to the bottom and begin to rise smoothly, the oil is hot enough. If they stay at the bottom or don't sink at all, the oil is not hot enough.

Place a few doughnuts at a time into the hot oil. Don't crowd them. Fry each batch for 2–3 minutes, turning them over from time to time until they turn dark golden brown.

Remove using a slotted spoon, drain them on kitchen paper/paper towels and either roll them in cinnamon sugar or serve them with maple syrup. That's the way we like to do things in Canada.

It's a bun. Enjoy it.

Index

Acknowledgments

My thanks to the entire team at Ryland Peters & Small for taking a punt on me again. And to all of the Bread Angels, Virtuous Bread students and The Real Bread Campaign for their inspiration and support.

For further information visit the following websites:
www.breadangels.com
www.virtuousbread.com
www.sustainweb.org/realbread